CODE OF PERSUASION

Chronicles of Influence in Life

By

Cary O. Goodwin

i

About the Author

Cary O. Goodwin's inspiring life a self-help author is well anchored in her great experience in psychology, making her have a different point of view about personal development and self-discovery. Her dedication in helping others is very present in her writing, in which she challenges readers on a transformative journey to self-acceptance and empowerment.

Goodwin's style is the harmony of good advice blended with compelling storytelling. She knows change is not always easy, but she is undeterred, and that gives her an edge: her profound insights, honed over the years in research and experience, illuminate the path to a more authentic life.

It is compassion that has made Cary O. Goodwin shine truly as one of the best in self-help books. She goes out of her way with empathy for each reader as she recognizes that every human being is unique, thus tailoring her guidance specifically to meet each reader's needs. Her knowledge thus becomes a light in the tunnel for the person who is desperately seeking himself and his positivity.

Cary O. Goodwin is the dear mentor in a world full of self-doubt and uncertainty, but through her wisdom and compassionate approach, she becomes a perfect companion on the path of self-realization toward a more empowered, authentic life. Her continued presence in the self-help arena remains a beacon of light for those navigating the sometimes challenging but ultimately rewarding journey of personal growth.

Table of Contents

About the Author ii

Chapter 1 Discovering the power of Persuasion 1

The Evolution of Persuasion through the Ages: A Journey across Time 2

Chapter 2 Foundation of Ancient Wisdom 5

Glimpses of Greek Mastery in Persuasion 5

Chinese Wisdom: The Art of Tacit Persuasion 9

Negotiation Tactics through the Ages 13

Chapter 3 Ethical Frameworks in Persuasion 20

The Rise of Ethical Persuasion 20

Examples of Ethical Persuasion in Marketing 23

A Theory That Backs Up Modern Enhancement of Persuasion 26

Chapter 4 Applying Persuasion in Modern Times 31

Modern Concepts in Persuasion 31

Applying Ancient Persuasion to Modern Business 34

Leadership influence: Impacting Others Positively 36

Applying Persuasion to Self-Development 38

Creating a ripple effect of positive influence within teams 40

Chapter 5 Persuasion in Business: From Sales to Wealth Multiplication **44**

Strategies for scaling businesses and achieving wealth multiplication *44*

Chapter 6 Navigating the Fine Line: Influence vs. Influence51

Balancing ethical practices with persuasive effectiveness...53

How to Use Persuasion for Individuals Like 1:1 Influencing *55*

Chapter 7 Creating Lasting Positive Impact **61**

Real-life examples of influential persuasion *62*

Strategies for leaving a lasting positive impression on others69

Chapter Eight Persuasion Alchemy in the Digital Age **77**

Adapting Ancient Wisdom to Modern Communication Trends78

Leveraging Digital Platforms for Ethical Persuasion *82*

Chapter Nine Emerging Trends and Persuasion **87**

2. Data-Driven Personalization *88*

3. Behavioural economics and nudge theory *88*

4. The Power of Social Media Influencers *89*

5. Immersive Technologies: VR and AR *90*

6. The Rise of Micro-Influencers *90*

7. Ethical Considerations and Transparency *91*

Chapter Ten Mastering Persuasion: A Lifelong Journey 93

Developing a Lifelong Commitment to Mastering Persuasion93

Continual Growth in Influence and Positive Impact.............95

Activity Session: Implementing Persuasion in Business Plans96

Concluding thoughts by the Author.................................. 100

Chapter 1
Discovering the power of Persuasion

Imagine a world in which persuasion was not about winning some debate or sealing some deal but about building actual relationships that create meaningful change. Just imagine every single interaction is going to create a difference, guided by empathy and a sense of understanding for how our words and actions matter. So, come on this transformational journey of discovering holistic persuasion: real connections and positive impact.

Pretend that you really want your friends to come with you to that charity event held locally. In this case, not being just persuasive enough as it is with that sort of event, you should tell them how such an opportunity to volunteer will make their lives more fun and filled in the future. You further explain to them how their participation could make a difference in the community-from helping needy people to creating a spirit of unity among volunteers. You are encouraging genuine enthusiasm based on emotion and values.

Holistic persuasion considers the reality that influence does not depend on agreement. Rather, it's making permanent and mutually beneficial changes to your own benefit. This happens when you take the interests, aspirations, and desires of the ones you desire to influence in order to create messages appealing to those interests. Building trust; cultivating genuine connections and, ultimately, granting the liberty to make choices in tandem with values and aspirations.

Let's consider a company trying to make consumers adopt eco-friendly products. Instead of just splashing them with numbers and statistics about environmental gains, it takes a much more holistic approach. The company writes compelling content teaching the consumer about the negative effects of their choices to the environment while also using the same content to draw out personal benefits, such as healthier lives and a healthy legacy for future generations. It thus appeals to reason and emotion, making for a strong argument.

At the most basic level, holistic persuasion is more than simple selling or artful persuasion - it's forging connections and catalyzing change while leaving an indelible mark on our world. Along this path, we will discuss principles and strategies behind holistic persuasion in numerous real-life contexts translated to benefits for people, organizations, and society at large. Let's begin the path that translates influence into action.

The Evolution of Persuasion through the Ages: A Journey across Time

1. *Ancient Persuasion*: Persuasion is an art whose roots are traced back in ancient civilizations, when skills of oratory were fundamental and essential. In ancient Greece, the great Aristotle took time to explore rhetoric-an art that emphasizes persuasion as a method of using logo, pathos, and ethos. Ancient Romans also used Cicero's rhetorical principles to guide them in persuasive communication that created the ground for developing effective methods of persuasion.

2. Medieval period Persuasion, during this period, sounded very religious. Clerics were influential in spreading persuasive theology and printing increased the proliferation of persuasion literature. Inflation of opinion became equivalent to a spread of a written message.

3. *The Renaissance and Enlightenment:* During the Renaissance, the interest in classical rhetoric increased and was used to make methods of persuasion more fine-tuned. In the Enlightenment, the focus of reason and logic was, therefore, also reflected in persuasion techniques. The political pamphlet and the writings started playing an important role in the formation of public opinion and became more pluralistic and pervasive in the process of persuasion.

4. *The Industrial Revolution:* The Industrial Revolution led to many changes in the society and communication. For example, mass production provided the means to distribute more effective messages because of newspapers. Persuasion would eventually incorporate pictures because of the advancement of advertising and propaganda.

5. *Communication in the 20th Century:* Persuasion evolved through several means of media in the 20th century. The radio and television came forth as primary means of persuasive communication. This led the political leaders, advertisers, and public figures to get their messages across to enormous audiences. Psychological theories from Freud and later on through behaviorists influenced the means of persuasion by looking towards emotional and subconscious triggers.

6. *Digital Age and Social Media:* The digital age and the advent of social media have really brought a revolution into persuasion, especially during late 20th and early 21st century. The Internet has enabled the interactive method of communication allowing two-way dialogues; it ushered in highly influential platforms of persuasion for social networking sites that accelerated the circulation of real-time information rapidly and molded

opinion in society.

7. *Personalization and Data-driven Persuasion:* The new world of persuasion is focusing on the practice of personalization in the present approaches. Right from the advertisers to marketers, through data analytics, this medium of communication is attuned to the individual preference and behavior. This appeal based on data makes persuasive communication all the more relevant and successful for the information-overload situation in modern times.

8. *Ethical Dimensions and Conscious Persuasion:* The ethical dimension has been part of the evolution of the discipline of persuasion. A persuader today in the modern era is conscious of the need for clarity, honesty, and responsibility in his or her communication. The conscious persuader is aware of the influence such persuasion may have on people and society, demanding an ethical responsibility.

It not only represents a change in communication media but also marks a change in the societal values, technology, and the understanding of human psychology. From ancient rhetoric to digital times, persuasion has undergone a process of adaptation and self-molding according to the changes in the landscapes of human interaction.

Chapter 2
Foundation of Ancient Wisdom

We'll dig into the past to discover how folks like the Greeks and Chinese used words and negotiation to get what they wanted. Think of it as a trip back in time to learn their tricks.

Glimpses of Greek Mastery in Persuasion

More than two thousand years ago, one of history's most recognizable philosophers Aristotle (384-322 B.C.E.) shed new light for us into the universe through his thinking. Among the insights that continue to be timeless is one: the essence of persuasive speaking. Despite living in a time when the universe's knowledge was more limited, Aristotle identified the "three appeals" that constitute persuasive communication. These timeless principles continue to be harnessed by persuaders across various domains, even in the realm of User experience design, as we strive to connect with users.

The Trio of Persuasion

Examining situations where a speaker aims to convince others, we often encounter someone presenting an argument. Whether it's a debate in school or a sales pitch on TV, persuaders articulate their case to influence an audience to take specific actions. The persuader requires a clear objective, a defined audience, and an effective way to convey their message to that audience. Crucially, their goal is to persuade rather than simply instruct, as noted by Aristotle, who outlined three essential components of the art of persuasion.

1. Logos – Appealing to Logic
2. Pathos – Appealing to Emotions
3. Ethos – Appealing to Ethics, Morals and Character

In the aspect of logos, a persuader relies on facts, statistics, quotes from reliable sources or experts, and what is already known. This part of the argument stands on solid evidence, demonstrating its strength based on factual information. They depend on the audience's intellect and reasoning to agree with their arguments and the final message. When speakers can persuade their audience that the message they are trying to put forth is the only choice and is logical, it shows that they have correctly applied the concept of Logos.

Within rhetoric, ethos is the role of the writer (speaker) in the argument and the credibility of the speaker's argument. This involves how knowledgeable or wise the speaker is about their argument and how morally reputable they are in the eyes of their audience. Aristotle called this "persuasion through character," as ethos primarily explores the characteristics of the speaker. Etiquette is also essential in developing an effective ethos, including proper use of tone, word choice, and respect for the views of the audience.

Instead of just translating to "logic," logos refers to the content of an argument and its organization. It involves forming meaningful connections between facts, supporting claims with evidence, and using analogies to create logical connections between ideas[1]. While ethos and pathos relate to the human qualities of the speaker and audience, logos primarily focuses on the characteristics of the argument itself in both its structure and presentation.

---

[1] *St. Louis Community College Writing Center. "Pathos, Logos, and Ethos." Accessed 3 May 2022.*

Consider structuring our appeals within a narrative framework for a water purification company. Let's say our storyline revolves around the Smiths, Joneses, and Johnsons, who are all concerned about the quality of their water supply and are eager to address the issue but feel uncertain about where to begin.

As a designer, you have various strategies for crafting your appeals. You could highlight the impressive efficacy of your water purification models by emphasizing that they capture 99% of pollutants, appealing to logic. Alternatively, you might opt for an emotional hook to evoke a sense of urgency among users, prompting them to seek out factual information. For instance, you could initially underscore the potential risks associated with unknown contaminants in water and then showcase how your company has successfully resolved similar issues for countless households. Injecting humor, such as making light of the journey water takes through various sources before reaching the tap, can also engage users emotionally (pathos).

Furthermore, it's crucial to establish credibility and expertise (ethos) by showcasing why your company is well-equipped to address water purity concerns.

However, before proceeding, it's essential to consider the audience. Understanding their needs, preferences, and concerns is paramount. Even with a compelling argument and well-crafted presentation, persuasion may fail if it doesn't resonate with the intended audience. Just like a comedian struggling with a hostile crowd, persuaders must ensure they are targeting the right audience to achieve success.

If you had to explain the benefits of drinking filtered water to both 7-year-olds and school administrators, your approach would differ. For the kids, you'd create a simple, image-heavy, and entertaining design, focusing on visuals to convey the message. However, for the school administrators who are concerned about costs and benefits, you'd opt for a more text-heavy presentation. This would involve detailed statistics, relevant images like diagrams, and a more serious tone to address their specific considerations.

The essence of your design is molded by your audience. Pinpointing your audience and establishing a sense of trust is pivotal. The ultimate aim is to captivate them to the extent that they not only comprehend but also feel compelled to take action. This could be whether marketing a product or offering a service, gaining approval is the bottom line. Imagine water purifiers, designing to cater to the public sphere.However, what if your industry lacks inherent appeal? Picture designing for a funeral director's business. Here, you're catering to a distinct user base—bereaved individuals and professionals in related fields. Irrespective of the industry, comprehending your audience is fundamental for crafting impactful designs.

The Power of Culture

While we may overlook it, culture is a crucial factor when understanding our audience. Despite the internet connecting us globally and increasing awareness of different cultures, our values are still significantly influenced by our cultural backgrounds. For example, what symbolizes mourning in one culture might represent purity in another. With a multitude of diverse cultures worldwide, what resonates positively in one may be offensive in another.

Hence, designing to cater to everyone is an impossible task. While opting for a neutral approach may seem like a safe choice, it poses a challenge as it lacks the power to deeply engage anyone. It's akin to painting rental property walls magnolia and installing beige carpeting – a choice that might not offend but won't leave a lasting impression. Congratulations on adopting a safe yet marginal approach that may not make your users feel entirely at home.

To stand out and captivate your users, you must evoke strong, positive emotions. This is the art of aiming for persuasive design, the flip side of the coin.

Aristotle outlined that persuasion involves a blend of three appeals: logos, pathos, and ethos. To effectively persuade an audience, one must incorporate facts (logos), appeal to the emotional aspect of an argument (pathos), and demonstrate moral standing (ethos), which includes professional intelligence, virtuous nature, and goodwill.

While crafting persuasive designs is essential, it's only one aspect of the equation. Success requires aligning designs with the right audience and considering cultural and lifestyle factors. Understanding the users is crucial. In UX design, the persuasive process begins by establishing trust through presenting ethos. Subsequently, presenting solid facts and strategically placed emotional hooks can capture users' interest.

*A character may almost be called the most effective means of persuasion."—**Aristotle***

Chinese Wisdom: The Art of Tacit Persuasion

Throughout Chinese history, there exists a wealth of records detailing persuasive communication practices, particularly during the Pre-China Autumn-Spring and Warring States period (770-250BCD). During this era, it was common for persuaders, known as "shuike meishi," to travel from state to state, offering their services to rulers or lords. Armed with eloquent speeches, they would present their political strategies to the ruling elite. This practice, known as "youshui" (traveling around to persuade) and "jinjian" (offering opinions to the ruler to do what is right), has become deeply ingrained in Chinese political tradition. Despite its prevalence, a notable absence of scholarly documentation studies this practice as a distinct subject. It seems illogical that in over two thousand years of Chinese civilization, no scholarly attention has been given to such a fundamental aspect of communication. However, ancient scholars, up to 280AD, extensively studied persuasion, albeit indirectly, as part of other subjects such as politics, government, or philosophy.

The ancient school of Chinese philosophy known as "mingbian" (name argument) scholars provides evidence of ancient scholars' academic interest in persuasion. These scholars specialized in various philosophical topics and were particularly interested in the logic of arguments. Consequently, persuasion and argumentation were crucial tools in their inquiries. Similarly, persuasion skills were essential for presenting and advocating political positions in government and politics.

Traditionally, the study of persuasion or rhetoric was conducted as complementary to other scholarly endeavors. It served as a means to comprehend human nature, governance, and the corresponding cosmic order. While it was never the primary focus of these studies, persuasion remained integral, as scholarly exchanges and political discussions necessitated clear presentation and argumentation. Both in academic and political contexts, effective communication and persuasion were vital for influencing opinions and actions. This longstanding emphasis on persuasion is evident in the extensive vocabulary related to persuasive activities found in ancient texts.

Related Vocabulary

The Chinese language offers a rich vocabulary for describing persuasion. According to Lu (1998), in classical Chinese, there were at least six terms specifically used to talk about persuasion, each with its unique meaning:

1. **Yan (言)**: This referred to using smooth talk to influence a ruler or to make political arguments that would have a certain impact. It could also include using language that showed political ambition, cultural training, or words that stirred up discontent with authority. It was all about trying to persuade someone directly or indirectly.

2. **Ci (辭)**: Similar to yan, this word was about using language, whether spoken or written, that was elegant and refined to have a certain artistic effect. The beauty of the language made the speaker or writer more credible and, therefore, more persuasive. However, it could also refer to people using fancy language to hide that they didn't have much substance behind their words, which could either make them famous or give them a bad reputation.

3. **Jian (諫)**: This was a specific type of persuasion done by officials to persuade a ruler to change a previous decision or to correct a mistake, for the benefit of the state and its people. It usually involved people of lower status trying to advise those of higher status. Whether it was successful often depended on whether the ruler was open to advice from their advisors. Sometimes, it was more effective when done by a group of people who shared a common viewpoint.

4. **Shui (說)**: This was about persuasion between equals or from someone to a ruler, usually about political or military matters. It was usually done by people who were wise or very knowledgeable.

5. **Ming (名)**: This wasn't directly about persuasion but about naming things, either as a verb or a noun. It was more about setting the moral rules for what was considered proper and acceptable in persuasion activities.

6. **Bian (辯)**: This was about making distinctions and teasing out differences through description. It was important in debates about the pros and cons of something, particularly in political matters. In scholarly contexts, it was about clearly defining related ideas. Today, it means to debate in modern Chinese.

Each of these terms represented different aspects of verbal persuasion in ancient China, and while they sometimes overlapped, they were never exactly the same. To understand their full meanings, you had to look at them in context and compare them to each other. Together, they gave a pretty comprehensive picture of how persuasion was understood in traditional Chinese culture.

Ancient Chinese culture highly valued actions and behavior as a more powerful form of persuasion compared to verbal communication. Proverbs such as "No attendance, no doing, no one believing" emphasized the importance of demonstrating actions to gain trust. Similarly, the saying "Act in righteous manner, others follow without order; act not in righteous manner, others will not follow even ordered" underscored the persuasive power of leading by example.

In contrast to mere words, fine deeds were believed to have a deeper impact on people's hearts. Actions were seen as more convincing than words, as expressed in the statement, "Fine talks do not go deep into heart as do fine deeds." This belief was further elaborated in the idea of "talk with acts and no words," where actions spoke louder than words. This faith in the power of action as persuasion extended to discussions about action itself, with persuaders often citing examples of others' actions as persuasive tools.

Furthermore, individuals frequently employed their own actions and experiences as analogies to persuade others, a practice known as "self-example persuasion." For example, Zouji, an official serving a Qi king, used his own experience of seeking honesty from his wife, concubine, and guest to persuade the king to recognize the importance of receiving truthful feedback. Similarly, a wet nurse in the Han Dynasty successfully persuaded Emperor Han Gaozhu to allow her to stay by demonstrating her reluctance to leave through her actions, effectively appealing to the emperor's emotions and sense of compassion.

In a nutshell, ancient Chinese culture valued actions over words in persuasion, recognizing the profound impact of leading by example and employing personal experiences as persuasive tools.

Negotiation Tactics through the Ages

The ancient civilizations have many negotiation tactics that are still alive today. One of these strategies came from ancient China, whereby the negotiators used the "win-win" tactic. The "win-win" tactic is a finding that will benefit both parties instead of just one party. The other strategy used from ancient Rome is the "divide and conquer" method. This involves breaking down a large group into small units to negotiate with individuals. One such strategy is the "Socratic method" from ancient Greece, which is questioning to find out the interests and motives of each party. Here are just a few examples of negotiation tactics from ancient times that still work today.

Yes, some more negotiation tactics from the ancient world:

"Tit for Tat" Ancient Mesopotamia It is called reciprocity. You react to the other side in exactly the manner in which they have reacted to you. If they give in or compromise, so do you. If they are hostile or uncooperative, so are you. The point is that you arrive at a just outcome and you facilitate cooperation.

"Silence" (Ancient Egypt): In old Egyptian negotiations, silence is the most potent tool. The silent negotiators would make the opponent uncomfortable and keep on applying pressure to make the opponent break the silence by offering some concessions or extra information. Silence can be used to gain an upper hand by making the other party talk, and it leaves them vulnerable as they open themselves up.

"Patience" (Ancient India): The practice of patience was the most emphasized in ancient Indian negotiation practices. Negotiators were not supposed to hurry and make any impulsive decisions. If the other party was willing to close the deal, patience would help the negotiator get better terms out of the deal. This is because patience gives the negotiator time to analyze the situation better and maybe even find some unexpected benefits.

"The Law of the Marketplace" (Ancient Greece): Derived from the school of thought from Greek philosophers, the technique is founded upon market price valuation of what should be negotiated.

14

Some prior research and analysis into existing market rates, demands, and supplies would need to be done in anticipation of a negotiation session. It may help the negotiator in making sound judgments or choices and negotiating consequently.

"Face-Saving" (Ancient East Asia). While in many ancient East Asian societies, it is a maxim to maintain the preservation of face or reputation, hence, to present oneself respectable, to remain dignified, and never to conduct oneself in an act, which might shame or ridicule the opposite side. While focusing on saving face could create an even more cordial and fruitful negotiation.

It is important to modernize these tactics and take into account ethical considerations in the use of negotiation strategies. While the ancient tactics are valuable, they must be combined with contemporary negotiation principles and adapted to the specific circumstances of each negotiation.

Practical Lessons from the Past

Lessons drawn from the pragmatic aspect of ancient techniques of negotiation and applied to today's contexts can teach lessons about effective persuasion strategies. When breaking down real-life examples into historical contexts, one can distill timeless principles that remain pertinent in the present. Let's talk about it in some detail on how we can learn from the past:

1. **Understanding Cultural Contexts:** Negotiation art in the past times is greatly affected by the dominant culture and value systems of those days. The learning experience through historical negotiations enables understanding the different cultural contexts prevalent in modern-day negotiation practices. For example, while some cultures like straightforward communication, others prefer subtlety and

indirect negotiation techniques. Knowing this will be helpful in making the right rapport and gaining some level of trust with counterparts from different cultural backgrounds.

2. **Relationship Building Factor:** In ancient techniques for negotiation, there was more focus on the long-term relationship-building factor rather than the short-term benefits. Nowadays, a genuine relationship building with the stakeholders will help in developing collaborative and mutually beneficial outcomes. With respect to the time and efforts invested in relationship building, we can lay the foundation for successful negotiations and future cooperation.

3. **Persuasive Communication Skills**: Greek speakers were known for skilled applications of persuasive communication: ethos, pathos, and logos. These same principles are applicable to present-day persuasion, be it business negotiation, a speech, or interpersonal conversation. Mastering the art of storytelling with deep evidence and appeal to emotions enables us to improve our capacity to persuade others effectively.

4. **Adaptive Strategies:** The old negotiators were flexible and adaptable to changing circumstances. Similarly, in modern times, the ability to pivot and adjust our negotiation strategies according to evolving dynamics can result in a successful outcome. Whether shifting tactics mid-negotiation or exploring alternative solutions, adaptability is key to overcoming obstacles and reaching mutually satisfactory agreements.

5. **Integrity and Ethics:** In using the attractive techniques, the ancient negotiators did maintain ethics and integrity. Similarly, in the present day negotiations, honesty, transparency, and

ethical practices are a must because these build credibility and trust. Being on high moral grounds, we can strengthen relationships, reduce conflicts, and ensure the results last long.

6. **Continuous improvement and learning:** Finally, you learn from historical negotiation cases and keep improving by fine-tuning your skills and methods. You can pick an area of improvement reading about the successes and failures based on past experiences. One develops more effective negotiation tactics with a growth mindset when one is open to different types of feedback. So, there is adaptation towards innovation and one becomes a master negotiator over time.

All of these boiled down to cultural understanding, the importance of building relationships, mastery in the persuasive use of communication, flexibility, integrity, and constant learning. These age-old principles, applied to our present situation, further polish our skills in persuasion toward success in life's numerous dimensions.

Ancient Principles Applied to Modern Times

Applying ancient wisdom to modern situations involves knowing that the insights of history stand the test of time but need to be adjusted so that they fit the situations of the present. Through this, we can infuse a touch of antiquity with a dash of modernity by combining past wisdom with present strategies. A comprehensive discussion on adapting and applying historical persuasion techniques in modern society is made below:

Understanding Human Psychology: The key human psychology concepts on which early forms of persuasion were founded often consisted of aspects such as appealing to emotions, demonstrating credibility, and applying the use of logic when making contact with others. Indeed, knowing human psychology is still highly relevant today and continues to influence the molding of choices and actions. Using one or more of these ideas - social proof, reciprocity, cognitive biases - in conjunction with others makes a message far more compelling and effective for influencing others.

Improving the Art of Communication: Rhetoric and Persuasion in Ancient Times and Its Relevance to the Modern World. Ancient civilizations placed a high premium on the art of rhetoric, the ability to persuade with eloquence. In modern life, effective communication is vital in professional and personal relationships, such as in negotiation, presentation, or personal interactions. The learning of ancient rhetorical techniques adapted to modern communication platforms allows people to improve their communication of ideas, rapport, and persuasion.

Building Relationships and Trust: The core component of traditional negotiation tactics is building relationships, especially where harmony and trust are the pillars, as in a Chinese culture. Today, genuine connection with stakeholders is a foundation of a successful deal. A person who, in all interactions, remains transparent, respectful, and empathetic, builds closer relationships and is able to navigate through intricate transactions easily.

Embracing Adaptability and Resilience: Early negotiators were flexible and resilient in handling the toughest of times. Today, the business world changes at such speed that flexibility, innovation, and overcoming the problem will help achieve success. The inspiration of resilience and perseverance by looking at history will help people to think more adaptively and be more resilient in a dynamic situation and overcome adversity.

We will proceed with various concrete examples of the two areas- namely companies and personal growth as to how techniques used centuries ago were adapted for usage in current times in subsequent chapters.

Chapter 3
Ethical Frameworks in Persuasion

The Rise of Ethical Persuasion

When people think of "persuasion," they often summon up the image of a stereotypical cheesy salesman - someone dressed in a plaid jacket, shiny shoes, and a forced smile, complete with an unappealing mustache. Their opening line usually rotates around appealing you with an apparently too-good-to-be-true offer.

However, this image is more about being distasteful than about genuine persuasion. None of us want to have such a negative stereotype of being associated with people like that. While clearly this is unethical to promise people something that is just out of reach, I claim that it is no more ethical to deny helping a person who really needs that help if you're actually able to do it.

Discovering what individuals truly desire and granting them permission to pursue it is key. So why do people require persuasion? The answer is twofold. Firstly, many individuals struggle to acknowledge their own needs due to low self-worth. Secondly, they fear making decisions, often stemming from this same lack of self-esteem.

Chances are, many of your customers, potential customers, and team members grapple with decision-making anxiety. They fear being wrong and being held accountable for their choices. As a leader, how can you support them? How can you encourage them to say "yes" without resorting to cheesy sales tactics? How can you help them move past indecision?

The solution lies in ethical persuasion. Ethical persuasion combines the art and science of guiding individuals off the fence. It involves empowering those you serve to feel confident in their decisions because, as Peter Drucker and others have noted, "Nothing happens until someone sells something."

You might argue that you're not in sales, but consider this: Have you ever needed to convince your team to embrace an idea? Requested a promotion or raise? Encouraged your children to go to bed? In each scenario, you were engaging in persuasion.

Every day, we engage in selling. While we may not trade physical goods, we trade ideas and beliefs. CEOs sell their vision to their organization, doctors sell treatments, and teachers sell the value of learning. Partners sell each other on marriage counseling, and friends sell each other on watching a movie or TV series.

Though we may not perceive ourselves as salespeople, every exchange involves a form of persuasion. Whether the currency is money or something intangible, the key is ensuring both parties feel good about the outcome. Finally, it is a matter of whether ethical or unethical persuasion had been exercised in the exchange.

Indeed, persuasion is an art and a science that plays an extremely important role in marketing. It is that superpower that creates value for customers and fuels the growth of brands. And yet it is something that needs to be understood-that persuasion is not one-size-fits-all; it requires deep understanding of our audience's needs, motivations, and emotions underpinned by ethical principles honoring customer autonomy and dignity.

Ethical use of persuasion in marketing is important; it may be either for good or bad outcomes. With ethical persuasion, one will act positively, leading to proper decisions about him and his life in conjunction with his set goals and principles. This is as opposite to unethical persuasion when done, the person buying does not need it and engages in unhealth practices by losing trust and breaking a brand name.

These means of ethical persuasion will not only call for respect, but also respect towards one's customers and well being. The principles include:

1. **Get to know your audience:** You need to know concerning the desires, concerns beliefs and motivations of the customers before you persuade. By this, you get tailored campaigns based on the respective needs and preferences.

2. **Value to customers:** Give customers value without trying to hoax them by mere smokescreen or deceptive claims. Avoid coercive harassment or fear sale and be straightforward and candid.

3. **Transparency:** Not conceal anything necessary about the product; linguistic and pictorial fraud can mislead the customer. Transparency establishes a belief in the brand in natural circumstances and continues to hold onto the relationships of the customer for longer periods of time.

4. **Respect for Autonomy:** Respect the independence of customers and not using any form of compulsion or exploitation of customers' cognitive weaknesses or their emotional vulnerabilities. Prioritize their autonomy in decision making.

5. **Consent:** Obtain explicit consent to collect or use customer information, respect their privacy preferences, and avoid unsolicited communication, and ensure they can control their information.

6. **Accountability:** Take responsibility for your actions and decisions, acknowledging mistakes and rectifying any harm caused. Accountability builds trust and reinforces brand integrity.

Examples of Ethical Persuasion in Marketing

Let's delve into details how brands implied ethical persuasion in their marketing strategies.

Patagonia's Sustainability Initiatives: Ethical persuasion is the core of Patagonia's sustainability programs in a bid to make stakeholders take environmental responsibility and social consciousness seriously. The company maintains openness about its supplier chain, environmental impact, and sustainability initiatives as a cornerstone of its business strategy in an effort to build consumer confidence and accountability. Another group that works towards conservation is informing its consumers of environmental issues through its website, social media, and advertisements. This equips consumers with knowledge to make good decisions. It has become a benchmark in the industry by being innovative about changing the process of its own business, such as the use of recycled materials in their products and less intake of water and energy. In addition to this, the organization connects with its communities in cooperation, meetings, and actions that call for social justice and environmental stewardship as a means to evoke shared responsibility and action. The group represents ethical persuasion by holding itself committed toward change of good nature to prompt a person's interest in assisting in making the future earth a better planet through volunteer experience, donations, and activist involvement.

Dove's Campaign for Real Beauty: The Dove campaign promoted women's self-esteem and confidence using a number of persuasion strategies. It used social proof and emotive appeals among others.

This is an appeal to emotions; this refers to a situation where a person convinces others to act emotionally. In the Dove advertisement, emotional appeals were used to create emotions of love, happiness, and confidence.

Heartwarming films and pictures of women with all body shapes and backgrounds embracing their inherent beauty were utilized in the campaign. The videos featured heartwarming scenes of moms teaching their daughters to accept themselves. The pictures showed ladies lovingly embracing their distinctive traits and showcasing their curves. No matter their size, shape, or skin tone, these emotive appeals were meant to inspire confidence and self-love in women.

Another kind of persuasion technique known as "social proof" is convincing people to do as their peers do. Social proof was used by the Dove ad to bolster women's self-esteem by demonstrating to them that they are not alone in their fears. In the campaign, a diverse range of women with varying life experiences, ages, sizes, and skin tones shared their individual tales of body insecurities. They discussed how seeing good images of themselves in the media had boosted their confidence and how they now accept their distinctive traits. Dove helped women who were having self-confidence issues feel connected to one another and supportive of one another by displaying strong testimonies from other women. This social proofing strategy sought to demonstrate to women that loving oneself is achievable and that it is okay to be different.

Apple's focus on privacy protection: The privacy protection of Apple forms one of the most significant elements of the ethical persuasion strategy. Apple focuses on protecting users' data and respecting the rights of privacy of the individual as a foundation for this strategy. This shows that the company communicates candidly with consumers about what privacy really means and all it does to safeguard their details. Apple equips its customers with privacy features such as biometric authentication, end-to-end encryption, and application permissions to personally manage their digital footprints and minimize the risks posed by data breaches and unauthorized access. The business regularly engages with industry stakeholders and legislators to support stronger privacy safeguards and improve digital security procedures globally. It also promotes for privacy laws and standards. The company is committed to privacy based on moral precepts of accountability, respect, and trust. This builds trust among consumers and loyalty as well as sets industry norms in responsible data stewardship. Apple's promotion of privacy as a basic human right in the digital era advances ethical persuasion while upholding user privacy through activities and activism.

The ethical argument for The Body Shop rests in its commitment to the cause of sustainability and welfare of animals.

Cruelty-free beauty is the core of the ideology, as proven by its long time stance against animal testing in the cosmetics industry. The Body Shop stands for a ban on animal experimentation and offers a lot of cruelty-free products in order to give customers the ability to make moral choices and live up to their value system. The Body Shop also shows commitment through a variety of programs by reducing their environmental impact. The company brings sustainability to every aspect of its business operations, as varied as it gets from ethical sourcing of natural ingredients to sustainable packaging and waste output. It engages with the customers concerning environmental issues and has transparent honesty regarding its sustainability initiatives in order to encourage an increase in environmentally friendly living.

Its conformity with animal welfare and the sustainability of the firm ensures the customers who have value for ethical and sustainable practices to trust and stick with The Body Shop. Excellent examples are not found in the beauty industry, especially in this kind.

The Body Shop successfully employs ethical persuasion to promote change and build a more caring and sustainable world by harmonizing its company principles with those of its clientele.

Ultimately, ethical persuasion is critical for trust-building, the formation of significant customer relationships, and for long-run success of a brand. Since it considers customer needs while showing regard for autonomy and authentic value creation, marketing can create a sound reputation and thereby gain sustainable growth in the highly competitive market.

A Theory That Backs Up Modern Enhancement of Persuasion

The Elaboration Likelihood Model (ELM) is theory idea that backs the modern enhancement of persuasion. The ELM, which Richard E. Petty and John Cacioppo developed in the 1980s, proposes that people perceive persuasive information in two different ways: centrally and peripherally.

The ELM offers insights on how people interact with persuasive content in a society that is becoming more digitally connected and digitally aware in the context of contemporary persuasion enhancement. Delivering persuasive messages to customers is made easier than ever thanks to the rise of social media, online advertising, and customized marketing tactics.

This pathway might be triggered in the modern digital environment when people come across convincing material that fits in with their interests, values, or worldviews. For instance, a well-researched essay or an engaging film may inspire people to evaluate the material and think about its consequences.

Conversely, the peripheral route of the ELM entails a more cursory analysis of persuasive signals, where people base their decisions on indications like competence, beauty, or social approval. Peripheral cues in the digital age can take many different forms, such as visually appealing visuals and design components, social proof indications (such likes and shares), or endorsements from influencers.

Overall, the ELM offers a theoretical framework for comprehending how contemporary communication channels and technology support both central and peripheral information processing pathways, thereby enhancing persuasion. Through the utilization of ELM insights, communicators, advertisers, and marketers can create more convincing strategies that are suited to the tastes and actions of modern audiences.

The following brands utilize the Elaboration Likelihood Model (ELM) in various ways to engage with consumers and influence their behavior:
1. **Apple:** Generally, the company applies high-involvement messaging in most of its advertisements by highlighting the quality, features, and benefits of the product (central route).

However, the company also applies peripheral cues such as celebrity endorsement and sleek design to draw more attention to its products and build positive associations with the brand.

2. **Nike:** Nike uses the central and peripheral route persuasions. Its advertisement often focuses on the performance and quality of its products as well as using emotional appeals, celebrity endorsements, and aspirational imagery to create positive attitudes toward the brand.

3. **Coca-Cola:** The peripheral route to persuasion is relied on by Coca-Cola as it associates its brand with happiness, friendship, and celebration through emotional appeals of advertisements. Although the central message of the ads can be very simple, like "Open Happiness," the peripheral cues of catchy jingles and uplifting imagery may play a big role in influencing attitudes toward the brand.

4. **Chanel:** The luxury brand Chanel, with very strong brand power and luxury products, uses the ELM to devise an attractive marketing strategy. The glamorous models and celebrities in the brand's ads evoke aspirational emotions, appealing to the consumer through peripheral processing. Besides, the brand focuses on the handcraftsmanship, heritage, and exclusivity of its products, appealing to the consumer's rational thinking, which triggers central processing.

5. **Amazon:** Amazon uses central and peripheral route persuasion strategies in its advertisements. It can be said that these campaigns are based on a lot of central route persuasion relating to the convenience, trustworthiness, and an array of products available on the platform. Peripheral cues including

reviews from customers, tailor-made suggestions, and privileges for being a Prime user incite consumer engagement and allegiance.

6. **Google:** Google marketers tend to give the central route factors as a way of showing their utility, relevance, and reliability of their product-be it search, email through Gmail, or their map service, Google Maps. But the corporation uses peripheral cues, such as the colors of the brandings, the friendly interfaces in using them, and industry specialists who support these to make them have even more credibility and acceptance.

7. **Pepsi:** Pepsi applies a periphery route of persuasion- celebrity endorsement, good and catchy ad campaign as well as sponsoring major events- like the Super Bowl. Thus even though the basic core may be on flavor as well as refreshment which may be the reason people seek a Pepsi, a consumer's activation on any or all of those routes adds to the good about a brand and thus away from the competition, as represented in this case, with the Coca-Cola.

8. **Nestle:** Nestle utilizes ELM by supporting peripherally presented arguments with some central arguments within the adverts. Nestle catches people's attention through colourful designs, creativity in slogans and endorsement through celebrities. Along with all this, it informs viewers about the nutrients and quality that will have a central approach towards reasonability.

9. **Starbucks:** This Company takes the central and peripheral route persuasions in its marketing process. Although quality, taste, and even personalization of coffee drinks are some of the

key aspects in their message (central route), the overall ambiance, corporate social responsibility, and even seasonal marketing strategies act as peripheral cues to attract customers and retain their business.

Chapter 4
Applying Persuasion in Modern Times

Modern Concepts in Persuasion

Isn't it true that, regardless of our roles—whether as salespeople, product managers, marketers, customer support managers, accountants, HR personnel, or even CEOs—the power to influence and persuade others to our way of thinking can be the defining factor in achieving success in business?

Whether the goals involve increases in sales, launch of new products or services to the marketplace, influence over company strategies, procedural changes, innovative work methodologies, or new market segments, it often depends on the ability to secure other's buy-in to the extent of one's success.

Originally, persuasion was perceived as some sort of art mastered only by those with either inherent charm or charisma. But Robert Cialdini, Professor of Psychology and Marketing, Arizona State University, persuasively sets the case that this is a science rather than an art, which operates through six universal principles.

His findings indicate that these principles can be learned systematically, practiced, and utilized to achieve desired ends in a professional sphere of activity.

In essence, Cialdini's findings represent a paradigm shift in recognizing that persuasive power is not inherently an art that flees and evades us but rather can be systematically studied, learned, and applied for one's purposes in an honest and ethical manner.

Persuasion is no longer something one does on instinct or intuition. Today we have available powerful strategies to persuade based upon six clear principles.

Even more astonishing is the reality that through leveraging these principles, we can make minor, frequently no-cost changes in our persuasion methods that have dramatic pay-off consequences. These strategies enable us to build profitable, positive, and durable relationships with others-whether they are customers, colleagues, employees, friends, spouses, or children.

So, what are these six principles, anyway according to Robert Cialdini?

Reciprocity: The principle of reciprocity takes advantage of the fact that humans reciprocate good deeds. Essentially, people are more likely to say yes to those who have previously said yes to them. Initiation of a gesture of goodwill, such as offering a small gift or favor, always invokes a feeling of obligation in someone else to reciprocate.

Scarcity: Human psychology dictates that people are more motivated by the fear of losing something than by the prospect of gaining it. Letting them know that they stand to lose something rather than gain it can drive action. This principle further creates a sense of urgency and exclusivity.

Authority: We tend to believe and accept what authority experts have to say about a specific issue. Authority or the impression of being an expert boosts our persuasiveness. Even showing credentials, experience, or endorsement can make all the difference in decision-making.

Consistency: People are always acting consistently, and their choices make sense in their own minds; thus, there is more likely to be adherence to commitments made in the past. By securing small, written commitments, we pave the way for larger agreements down the line. This principle taps into the fundamental human desire to keep things internally harmonious and consistent with previous actions

Liking: We say yes to people we like, and then there are three primary factors that go into likability: similarity, compliments, and cooperation. To build rapport and commonality breeds trust and cooperation. Finding common interests, giving genuine compliments, and creating mutual collaboration enhance not only our likability but also our persuasive influence.

Consensus: People follow others, especially those that are like them, in what to do and in their decisions. The fact that we display choices of like-minded peers increases the chance of obtaining an agreement because this principle relies on social proof and the human desire to go along with the group.

These principles are ethical if they are used authenticatively as well as appropriately in a given context. It involves identifying principles which can be leveraged and authentically exist within the context. However, masquerading as an expert or manufacturing consensus constitutes manipulation, and gradually erodes trust while damaging relationships in the long run.

What is interesting is that effective persuaders spend more time in planning their method from these principles rather than developing their offer alone. They carefully prepare the foundation using these principles as if a gardener will cultivate the soil before

33

seeding the plants.

Listening to Robert Cialdini gives insight into how to wisely use these principles, thus being more persuasive and creating good, moral relationships with many stakeholders.[2]

Applying Ancient Persuasion to Modern Business

Persuasion from sales to wealth multiplication is drawn from timeless principles that have been employed since ancient times. Studies of ancient persuasion methods and their resultant relevance and applicability in the modern business practices will serve as valuable insight into how successful businesses can influence their customers, partners, and stakeholders to achieve success and wealth multiplication.

Building rapport: Merchants in the traditional marketplace were known to engage with prospective customers in friendly conversation, demonstrating an interest in their lives and needs. Through personal relationships and empathy, merchants earned such customers' trust and loyalty. In this regard, a salesperson may utilize platforms of social media to engage with prospects by commenting on those posts and sharing relevant content. The salesperson can build rapport and create a positive relationship between the two parties by interplaying authentically and demonstrating an interest.

Creating Urgency: At an ancient bazaar, sellers would declare offers that were available for a certain period only or deals that the customer would get by visiting the shop. Customers were

---

[2] https://youtu.be/OwN3J1VytH4

motivated to purchase quickly before the offers closed. Today, with online retailers, a countdown timer or a notification that some items are of a limited stock may be used to create a sensation during sales. Emphasizing the scarcity of products or time-limited offers keeps motivating customers to make a quick decision to purchase.

Using Social Proof: In the old markets, customers with pleasant experiences shared their stories with friends and family, influencing others to shop from the same merchants. This word-of-mouth recommendation was an incredibly powerful form of social proof. Today also, an e-commerce portal could include customer feedback and ratings alongside products. This will tell potential shoppers about previous buyers' experience with the same products. Fresh feedback and good recommendations from satisfied customers breed credit and trust in the minds of prospective shoppers.

Utilizing Reciprocity: Merchants in ancient trade networks offered free samples or a gift to the prospective customers as a good will gesture. Generous gestures usually led to reciprocation, since such customers would have felt obligated to buy from the same merchants later. Nowadays, when there is a software company wanting to give prospective clients an experience of benefits, they use reciprocity by offering a free trial or demo of their product. By giving value first and demonstrating the worth of their software product, the company is nurturing reciprocity and conversion.

Win-Win Solutions: In the old days of contract negotiations, merchants and traders sought mutual agreements that satisfied both parties' need and interest. This way, through finding common ground and compromise on terms, they would get a positive outcome for everyone. Similarly, in contemporary business alliances, firms may collaborate in producing a joint promotional campaign marketing their complementary products. Both parties can benefit since the exposure of one will complementally increase another's revenue-generating chances in a win-win solution.

Using examples both from yesteryears and years from now illustrates how principles related to persuasion have transcended time, application venues, and contexts to manipulate and influence the attitudes and behaviors of the customers towards achieving successful and positive sales and negotiation results.

Leadership influence: Impacting Others Positively

1. Historical Source of Persuasive Leadership: In ancient world civilizations such as Greece and Rome, persuasion in communication was essential to get the backing, raise armies, and manage properly. Leaders like Pericles and Julius Caesar were known for their oratory skills and ability to move crowds with rhetorical speeches.

Connection to Current Leadership: More recent leadership theories, such as transformational leadership theory, emphasize the role of persuasion in motivating and inspiring followers. Contemporary leaders employ the same technique of persuasive communication that their ancient counterparts utilized to explain a vision, build consensus, and spur action.

Example: Winston Churchill, prime minister of the United Kingdom during the events of World War II, exemplified persuasive effective leadership in his speeches, such as the "We Shall Fight on the Beaches" speech, which he gave to rouse the people of Britain during a time of great crisis and induce them into acts of bravery.

2. Philosophical Foundations of Ethical Leadership: Aristotle and Cicero Ancient philosophers discussed the art of persuasion as well as its ethical implications. They focussed on the importance of ethos (credibility), pathos (emotion), and logos (reason) in persuasive discourse.

Connection to Modern Leadership: For the modern scholars of leadership, persuasion raises important ethical issues and deals with the aspects of trust and credibility. Real leaders build trust through principles of integrity, authenticity, and empathy toward their followers.

Example: Nelson Mandela, former President of South Africa, used ethical persuasion to take the entire nation out of apartheid and usher it into an era of democracy and reconciliation. His message of forgiveness and unity called people of all walks of life to respect and acclaim him everywhere

3. Psychological Insights in Persuasive Leadership: Ancient leaders frequently used psychological principles for opinion and behavior changes. They appreciated the effectiveness of emotional appeal, social proof, and biases in cognitive areas to shape opinions and mobilize support.

Connection to Contemporary Leadership: Psychological insights are used in contemporary leadership to augment persuasion and decision-making. The leaders use storytelling, social proof, and framing as tools to appeal to the emotion and motivation of followers.

Example: Steve Jobs, the co-founder of Apple Inc. He was famous for the presentation skill as well as his capacity to attract people with storytelling. His product launch, like the launch of iPhone in 2007, seamlessly amalgamated technical innovativeness with emotional storytelling to attract consumers' excitements and anticipation.

4. Cultural Adaptation of Persuasive Leadership: In Persuasive Leadership, ancient leaders tailored their persuasive strategies according to the cultural norms and values of their time. Messages were adapted according to varied audiences in such a manner that persuasion was context-specific, depending on factors like language, religion, and social hierarchies.

Today's leaders realize the urgent need for effective use of adaptability and sensibility in the culture while delivering persuasive communications. They let their messages conform to different cultural backgrounds and preferences to increase inclusion and effectiveness.

Example: Pakistani activist for girls' education and youngest Nobel Prize laureate, Malala Yousafzai uses persuasive communication highly respecting the cultural nuances of the targeted audience. Her messages, involving advocacy of girls' education, are heard throughout the world, yet contextualized about local cultural norms and challenges.

Applying Persuasion to Self-Development

Applying persuasion techniques may be one of the most powerful tools of personal growth and self-development. If persuasion is understood and applied appropriately, people can influence their own thoughts, behaviors, and actions to achieve their dreams. For instance, individual can overcome himself and develop confidence by using self-persuasion techniques such as positive self-affirmations and visualization. Persuasion can also be applied to motivates and commits individuals to achieving personal goals presented through attractive inspiring terms. Finally, gaining insight into the art of persuasion would also make one more persuasive in communication and hence a better influencer/inspirer in one's personal life as well as professional life. Thus, tapping into persuasion power can unlock individuals' powers and propel them meaningfully toward personal growth and fulfillment.

In the modern world, persuasive techniques for personal growth can draw inspiration from the ancient methods that have really stood the test of time. For example, rapport building, a principle frequently applied in sales and networking may have its origin in ancient marketplaces where merchants went out to engage in pleasant conversations in order to establish trust and loyalty. Today, one can build rapport through social media interactions, commenting on posts, sharing content to connect with others.

Another very ancient tactic of persuasion is creating urgency, which is used in modern marketing through limited-time offers and countdown timers. This plays into a deep human instinct to act when things are scarce and to keep one's own personal goals or aspirations from going unfulfilled.

Utilizing social proof-that is, a concept very deeply ingrained in ancient word-of-mouth recommendations-finds its modern counterpart in customer reviews and testimonials displayed prominently on e-commerce platforms. In this sense, by showing other people's experiences, an individual may influence his or her own decision-making processes and validate choices, thus facilitating personal growth and development.

Beyond that, the law of reciprocity, which was applied in old trade when traders shipped samples or gifts, may be cultivated within the new system to ensure doing good deeds for someone else. Returning to society in one way or contributing to other people's business may create good will and maybe reciprocity, which as said before contributes to a personal growth journey.

Overall, by understanding and adapting ancient persuasion methods to the modern world, individuals can effectively enhance their personal growth and development, leveraging timeless principles to achieve goals and aspirations in today's society.

Creating a ripple effect of positive influence within teams

Uncertainty surrounds the world today, making leadership play such an important role in ensuring that change is positive. Great or small, each act of leadership contains an immense possibility; as beautifully put by Mother Teresa, "I alone cannot change the world, but I can cast a stone across the water to create many ripples."

Since work and personal life are always interlinked, the negative and positive experiences we have outside of work are quite likely to affect our work performance and behavior. Positive experiences in personal life can further enrich professional aspects of life.

Leadership requires self-care and well-being; therefore, it's important to set an example for our team members. The exercise of taking care of ourselves sends the message regarding the value that should be attached to self-care within a friendly culture where the well-being of each employee is cherished.

Also, leaders support their team members during difficult times and provide them with the required aid and understanding to face and overcome those challenges. Supporting and empathizing with their team members not only helps individuals but also enables them to contribute better to the teams as well.

In the bigger picture of work, leaders have the power to drive positive change by aligning company policies with values, fostering inclusion, and driving sustainability. However, the influence of leadership also extends beyond just policies and initiatives; every action, from mentoring a colleague to promoting teamwork, has a ripple effect that ripples throughout an entire organization.
Positive leadership transcends a mere role; it is about resilience, empathy, and a growth mindset. Positive work environment encourages innovation, creativity, and productivity, which imply good business outcomes.

In the retail industry, positive leadership is critical, as it impacts the customer experience and business success directly. Transformative retail leaders motivate their teams to deliver better service while trying to create memorable experiences for customers and generating sales.

Self-awareness, emotional intelligence, and purpose are among the things that will drive the effectiveness of impactful leadership. The better one understands themselves and their influence on others, the more effectively he can lead with empathy, clarity, and inspiration to empower the team toward greatness.

Ultimately, positive leadership can lead to change in organizations and ripple across the globe beyond the workplace. It also empowers leaders to lead toward positive change and encourage others to do so in their actions to drive differences in the world.

In ancient societies like Greece and Rome, well-being was highly regarded. Leaders and orators used persuasive tactics to achieve consolidation of communities, stimulate collective action, and promote feelings of nationality among citizens. For example, in Athens, public forums were an open platform where the citizenry stated opinions and participated in processes that determined various decisions. This approach engendered democratic openness and cooperation just like emphasizing openness in communication and reaction in contemporary teams. Just as Athenian citizens were empowered by their ability to contribute to the common good, team members today thrive in environments where their voices are heard and valued.

Shared aims and values, too, were an emphasis of the classic philosophers, such as Aristotle, who said that speakers could win the hearts and minds of the audience by appealing to shared interests and ethical principles. Today's teams have a shared vision and a set of goals described by the leaders that suit the interests of every individual and motivate them with direction and purpose. A project manager can rally a team to a common end, such as delivering high-quality results to clients, emphasizing teamwork and excellence.

Leaders in ancient Rome also led by example, often exemplifying virtues such as integrity, courage, and sympathy. Their behaviors engender trust and loyalty among followers; the culture becomes one of respect for others and cooperation. The same applies for the modern leaders who live by good behaviors and values and, hence, become role models for those they lead. For example, a CEO who is known for demonstrating transparency, humility, and empathy on a regular basis in interacting with staff will, in turn, influence others to reflect his style of behavior and attitude.

In the historic and modern context, recognition and appreciation are fundamental instruments for motivating people and ensuring repeat of desired behavior. In ancient Rome, for example, military commanders were known to give rewards to soldiers for acts of bravery and valor, boosting morale and camaraderie among soldiers. Similarly, in modern teams, recognition and celebration of team member accomplishments foster a recognition and appreciation culture, encouraging them to continue to excel. For instance, a team leader might publicly thank an employee for offering a brilliant solution to a difficult problem by emphasizing that it supported the team and worked out positively.

Using the above examples of an analogy between ancient techniques of persuasions and modern patterns of teamwork and presenting them in organizational settings could be an effective way to apply timeless ideas that create positive, collaborative, and supportive work environments.

Chapter 5
Persuasion in Business: From Sales to Wealth Multiplication

Strategies for scaling businesses and achieving wealth multiplication

In the olden days, persuasion was of chief importance in different aspects of society, whether commercial, political or social. Most of the persuasion principles applied then are alive in modern business practices in scaling businesses and multiplication of wealth. Let's discuss how these ancient methods of persuasion relate to contemporary business practices:

1. Market Research and Niche Identification:

In early marketplaces, merchants relied on persuasive communication to seek knowledge regarding consumers' preferences and market trends. Persuasively asking customers questions, observing their buying patterns, and adapting their offerings would fulfill the demands created. Using persuasive communication, the modern-day businesspersons conducts market research by convincing customers to provide opinions through surveys, focus groups, and interviews. Through an understanding of consumer needs and preferences, businesses can identify profitable niches and produce appropriate products or services according to the specific needs of their markets.

Let's take the example of a tech startup searching the market for its newly launched software product. Persuasion depends on the self-interest of key players in that particular industry about the prospect of influencing future industry trends, thereby making them willing subjects of the surveys and interviews they offer. Persuasive communication assists a startup in finding out the customer preferences and pain points and thus entering into profit-generating niches.

2. Process Optimization and Operational Efficiency

The ancient political leaders and military strategists used persuasion in order to form an organizational design and streamline the processes for maximum efficiency.

They used to persuade the people and soldiers to work in routine patterns and strategic movement to reach the objectives. Hence, the business leaders today persuade employees to adapt new technology and workflows for optimum operational efficiency. By expressing the process optimization benefits, businesses can reduce unnecessary activities and increase productivity while saving on costs to enhance profitability.

For instance, a manufacturing business convinces its employees to adopt a new lean manufacturing process intended to promote no-waste processes and improve efficiency. In relating the potential benefits of the new process, such as increased productivity and reduced costs, to the workers that may initially resist change, the company gains buy-in. In this way, the business generates critical operational efficiency and profitability.

3. Scalable Business Model:

Ancient traders and explorers used persuasive storytelling to attract investors and to fund their expeditions.

They painted vivid pictures of untapped markets and potential riches and convinced the sponsors to provide the funds for their ventures. Modern entrepreneurs use persuasive pitches and business plans to attract investors and partners as a means of providing the needed capital for their growth initiatives. An entrepreneur can successfully gain the much-needed capital to scale up their operations in various markets by articulating a compelling vision and demonstrating the scalability of their business models.

To this end, an e-commerce startup convinces its investors to fund its expansion plans by accurately presenting its business model focused on scalability and profit generation. The startup effectively communicates the potential for rapid growth in the e-commerce market and convinces investors of the company's ability to capture market share. Getting funding allows the startup to execute its growth strategy and produce exponential revenue growth.

4. Strategic Partnerships and Alliances

During the olden times, alliances were forged through rhetoric and mutual benefits. City-states and kingdoms allied themselves to enhance their defense, expand their territories, and have free access to valuable resources. Similarly, the modern day business forges strategic alliances through rhetoric and alignment of interest. Through emphasizing common goals and mutual benefits, businesses can negotiate alliances that improve competition advantage and growth through teamwork.

For example, a software company makes a leading technology firm agree to sign an agreement on strategic partnership by emphasizing the synergies between their products and the mutual benefits of collaboration. Through negotiation persuasiveness, both firms agree to integrate their software solutions, thus creating an even more holistic offering to customers. The partnership hence strengthens the market positions of both firms while enhancing revenue in terms of sales volume as well as market penetration.

5. Customer Acquisition and Retention

Ancient merchants understood building trust and rapport with the customers in order to foster loyalty and repeat business. Ancient merchants use persuasive sales techniques and customer-experience individualizations to attract and retain customers. It has become easy for businesses of today to gain and hold customers through persuasive marketing messages and customer-centric strategies. Authentic interaction with customers and exceptional experiences culminate long-term relationships that drive loyalty and advocacy.

This service will entice its prospects to sign up with its platform by offering a free trial, demonstrating how valuable features and benefits are. Due to persuasive marketing messages and personalized outreach, the company is able to attract a large volume of users who have taken a trial to become a paying customer. All that is needed is a focus on customer satisfaction and a superior user experience to produce high retention rates and sustainable revenue growth.

6. Financial Planning and Investment

In ancient economies, persuasive rhetoric was used to secure loans, investment, and funding for commercial expeditions as well as state projects.

Lords persuaded financiers and donors to invest in projects that would bring economic benefits or serve the common good. In recent times, modern businesses make compelling pitches and financial projections to attract investors and raise funds for growth projects. Thus, presenting a compelling case for investment and potential returns motivates businesses to address the capital necessary for fueling expansion and innovation. A biotech startup convinces the venture capitalists to invest in its innovative research through a presentation of extremely attractive data regarding the probable therapeutic benefits that its drug candidates will have. The presentation of highly attractive pitches and scientific presentations convinced investors of the great market opportunity and high prospects of regulatory approval. After securing funding, the firm continuously developed its efforts on research and development and finally brought life-saving treatments to the market.

7. Constant Innovation and Innovation

The old people innovated through experimenting and adapting changes in the environment. The leaders managed to convince people to embrace new technologies and cultures in agriculture, which ensured the improvement of human life in society. In much the same way, innovation takes place in modern organizations, where inspiring leadership combined with an innovative culture motivates employees to experiment. Inspiring employees to take on change and to explore new ideas helps firms gain a market lead and innovation-based growth in the organization.

For example, a retailing company persuades employees to embrace the digital transformation by spreading the potential returns of technology adoption, more especially customer engagement and efficiency through operations. The company trains the employees through persuasive leadership by equipping them with the expertise of adopting new technologies as well as innovative solutions that meet customers' diverse needs in evolving circumstances. Consequently, the company will always remain in the run in the digital marketplace and continue increasing its market share even further.

8. Talent Acquisition and Development:

Persuasive leaders in ancient societies attract skilled artisans and craftsmen as well as advisors to their courts and workshops. The advancement and gaining of recognition made them a magnet, and they develop and foster cultures that nurture learning as well as mentorship to develop talent as well as reinforce loyalty. Businesses today compete with attractive employer branding and recruitment tactics. Businesses can appeal talented and best employees by promising competitive compensation as well as creating an empowering work environment through they will be driven to perform better.

For example, a fast-growth company acquires the best talent by offering highly competitive salaries, good benefits, and career opportunities. In so doing, it projects itself as an employer of choice through inviting recruitment efforts and employer branding initiatives. In doing this, the company capitalises in employee development and creates a positive work culture, keeping its talent on board while driving innovation and growth.

9. Risk Management and Contingency Planning

In olden times, the rulers and warlords used persuasive speech to assemble resources and garner support for defensive measures and contingency plans.

They convinced citizens and soldiers to be prepared for looming threats and disasters by preparing defenses and stockpiling provisions. Similarly, today's business organizations also use persuasive communication to secure support for a risk management strategy and contingency planning. In doing so, businesses can effectively circumvent threats and be ready for potential risks by communicating the need for awareness and preparedness about risk. Consider a financial services firm that convinces clients to diversify the investment portfolios by emphasizing the importance of risk management and asset allocation. Through well-articulated financial planning sessions as well as education seminars, the firm educates the clients on the dangers posed by concentrated investments and the benefits of spreading assets. The firm assists its clients in cruising through fluctuations in markets and freak incidents, and thus their wealth is saved and reaches long-term financial success.

Chapter 6
Navigating the Fine Line: Influence vs. Influence

Influence and impact are two of the very essential concepts involved in human interaction, though often understood yet holding different characteristics. This chapter will focus on differentiating between influence and impact along with their basic correlation to the concept of persuasion. Exploring examples through some of the best-known companies will also help better understand the operation of these concepts in any real context.

Differentiating Influence and Impact: Influence, as expressed through the example of companies like Apple, Google, and Coca-Cola, encompasses the power to influence consumers' perceptions, preferences, and behaviors. These brands use the branding concept, marketing tactics, and innovative products to influence consumer choices, thereby making them choose the desired product or service. Influence works on a proactive level, with the intent to influence behavior, whether that is through making people guide or manipulate behavior by using such measures as advertisements, brand messages, and customer experience designs.

Another facet of impact is seen in the tangible outcome or consequence that follows from an action or initiative by a company. Companies that have the power behind the play are demonstrated in companies such as Tesla, Amazon, and Patagonia, for sustainability, technological advancement, and social responsibility, respectively. Impact encompasses environmental stewardship, societal progress, and technological advancement besides financial metrics. Although influence focuses on the process of exerting control, impact centers on the outcomes or results achieved as a result of such influence.

Relating Influence and Impact to Persuasion: Influence and impact both necessarily involve a process of persuasion as an essential element that acts as a precursor to behavior change or realization of result. Companies like Nike, Airbnb, and Starbucks demonstrate the strategic employment of persuasion tools to influence consumer behavior toward the brand. Indeed, storytelling, emotional branding, and experiential marketing are some of the approaches being effectively used by such companies to persuade consumers to live up to these companies' values, preferences, or lifestyle.

Like persuasion, translation of influence into actual outcomes or results significantly contributes to the realization of impact. Companies such as Microsoft, IBM, or Facebook employ the power of persuasion in delivering social change through innovation and helping overcome global challenges. Corporate social responsibility initiatives, philanthropic activities, and advocacy actions are all examples of how persuasion is used by these companies to inspire action and mobilize stakeholders to bring about positive change in society.

Practical Examples: To exemplify the interconnectedness of influence, impact, and persuasion, consider the following scenario: Apple's persuasive marketing campaigns and innovative product designs influence consumer perceptions and preferences, driving demand for its products (influence). Subsequently, Apple's commitment to sustainability and renewable energy initiatives results in tangible environmental benefits, such as reduced carbon emissions and energy conservation (impact).

In a nutshell, influence and impact are two integral parts of corporate strategy that play exclusive yet interconnected roles in influencing consumer behavior and, ultimately, business outcomes. A firm grasping the difference between influence and impact and their intrinsic link to persuasion will be better positioned to engage consumers, drive social change, and strive for meaningful outcomes within the dynamic marketplace.

Balancing ethical practices with persuasive effectiveness

In today's business environment, where consumers demand transparency and social responsibility more and more, striking a balance between ethical standards and persuasive efficacy is essential. Let us examine several actual instances of businesses that have effectively struck this balance:

TOMS Shoes: Famous for the "One for One" shoe distribution program, where a pair of shoes is donated to a child in need for each pair sold. The foundation of TOMS' brand identity has been their humanitarian approach to business, which successfully influences customer choice while simultaneously having a good social impact. Customers that respect ethical behavior have overwhelmingly backed TOMS because of the openness and honesty communicated from the establishment of the humanitarian objective.

Ben & Jerry's: The legendary ice cream company has a long history of exercising social and environmental responsibility. Ethics are deeply ingrained into every part of Ben & Jerry's firm operations-from sourcing fair trade ingredients to promoting social justice issues. The company convinces people to believe in their brand not only because of its fantastic ice cream but also because of its approach to business rooted in values through strong marketing campaigns and activist actions.

IKEA: The renowned brand IKEA positioned itself as environmentally friendly, pledging to avoid, reuse, and recycle waste; increase renewable sources of energy, mainly from wind turbines; and source materials responsibly. Of note is the "People &

Planet Positive" strategy launched by IKEA, where the company makes ambitious commitments to make IKEA products even more environmentally friendly yet affordable to consumers. It would attract customers as the more environment-friendly choice by public communication of the sustainability transparency initiatives and offering them with options in eco-friendly selection choices.

On the other hand, adopting dishonest or manipulative strategies to achieve short-term gains at the price of moral values is a common example of how to balance ethical practices with persuasive efficacy gone wrong. The following examples show how unethical persuasive techniques can be used:

Companies can engage in deceptive forms of advertising to influence customers into purchasing their products. Such techniques may include false or exaggerated claims as regards the benefits of a given product, manipulative pricing schemes, or false marketing techniques designed to take advantage of consumer weaknesses.

Political spin and manipulation: Politicians and other influential people in society will use spin and manipulation in an attempt to influence public opinion and attain support for their goals. This can involve the fabrication of information, dissemination of falsehoods, or manipulation of fear to alter opinions. All of these tactics have adverse effects on public trust in political institutions and democratic processes.

Coercive sales tactics: To persuade customers to make a purchase, some salespeople use coercive tactics. Coercive tactics, such as strong persuasion, intimidation, and even emotional manipulation, can be used to make someone purchase a good or service against their better judgment.

Marketing ethical dilemmas: A marketer faces an ethical dilemma if a product or service has the unintended consequence of destroying society and its customers. These could include the risks of addictive products, the exploitation of vulnerable populations, or dishonest marketing strategies used to increase sales.

Influence peddling and bribery: In corrupt circumstances, persons or groups will use bribery or influence peddling to gain unfair advantage or influence judgments. This unethical behavior promotes nepotism and violates the integrity of institutions in a nation.

All things considered, these instances show the dangers of putting persuasive power ahead of morality. Persuasive strategies can backfire on people, institutions, and society when they turn toward manipulation, deceit, coercion, or corruption. Building trust, trustworthiness, and enduring relationships with their audience through compelling communication necessitates that individuals and organizations uphold ethical beliefs and values.

How to Use Persuasion for Individuals Like 1:1 Influencing

Using persuasion effectively in one-on-one interactions involves understanding psychological principles, employing strategic techniques, and genuinely engaging with the other person. Here's an in-depth guide on how to use persuasion in one-on-one interactions, supported by detailed examples from real life and renowned companies.

Principles of Persuasion

One of the primary persuasion principles is reciprocity or the idea that people often give back. If you do something positive for someone else, they probably will do something positive for you in return. For example, if you help your coworker complete his or her assignment, they may feel obligated to help you with yours sometime.

Commitment and consistency is the second principle of persuasion, which states that people like consistency with their previous actions and commitments. They are more likely to see through their commitments. You are more likely to be able to get a person to agree to a bigger request at a later time if you can first get them to agree to a smaller one. We call it the "foot-in-the-door" strategy.

The other influential principle is based on social proof; people look to others to determine how to behave. Showing people that many others are doing something can persuade them to do it too. For instance, where you tell your friend that many people have successfully adopted a new habit, they are more likely to try it.

Authority is equally important. People tend to follow the lead of credible and knowledgeable experts. For example, if a doctor recommends a particular health regimen, people are more likely to follow.

The third key principle is liking. It is easy to be convinced by a man who likes him. Building rapport can enhance this principle. A salesperson, for instance, who finds common interests with his client and builds a friendly rapport will likely make the sale because he likes that client.

Finally, scarcity is a great motivator. People are driven by the threat of losing more than they are inspired to achieve something of worth when equal. For example, whereas an offer or a one-time bargain creates a sense of urgency, it compels the person to act faster.

Techniques of Persuasion

Active listening is an essential technique. Show actual interest by paying attention, reflecting on what is being said, and responding thoughtfully. This generates trust. When negotiating, listening to the other party's concerns and alleviating those burdens contributes to achieving a more favorable outcome.

Building Rapport: t is important to build rapport. Connect on interests and through empathy. For example, a manager who listens to what an employee is interested in or what he hopes to achieve can more effectively motivate and influence his performance.

Framing the argument effectively: It is another key technique. When expressing your thoughts, make sure they align with the values and objectives of the other person. For instance, while attempting to convince someone to adopt a healthy lifestyle, emphasize the advantages they would experience on a personal level, such as being more energetic and living longer.

Using questions strategically: This technique can steer another person to your desired conclusion. For instance, instead of telling a friend to exercise more, ask, "How do you feel after you work out?" This makes them find the benefits for themselves.

Storytelling: Storytelling is a pretty powerful weapon in the game of persuasion. Share the most compelling stories that illustrate your point while making your argument more relatable and memorable. For example, to sell the new work method to a team, relate how another team had enjoyed success with the same change.

Presenting benefits is necessary. Discuss how a specific action will benefit the other person. For instance, when a new idea is proposed to a client, outline the optimistic outcomes they will gain from the proposed action, such as increased sales or market reach.

Real-Life Examples

Negotiating a Raise

Jane wants a raise at work and knows her boss values results and team cohesion. She starts by acknowledging the support her boss has provided and offers to take on an additional project to help the team (reciprocity). She reminds her boss of previous commitments to reward high performance and points out her achievements (commitment and consistency). Jane references industry salary standards and mentions advice from a career mentor (authority). Thus, by aligning her request with the values of the company and demonstrating a continued commitment, Jane is able to effectively persuade her boss to give her a raise.

Encouraging a Client to Sign a Contract

Tom is a sales representative who attempts to close a deal with a potential client. He cites testimonials from other satisfied clients who have benefited from his product (social proof). He establishes a rapport by finding common interests with the client and sharing relevant personal anecdotes (liking). Tom mentions a limited offer, stating that it would be available only for a limited time (scarcity). Encouraged by the experience of others who favor the deal, and also by his emotional attachment toward Tom, the client decides to sign the contract.

Encouraging Healthy Eating in a Child

A parent wants their child to eat more vegetables. They talk about how their favorite athletes eat vegetables to stay strong and healthy (authority). They tell a fun story about a superhero who gains special powers from eating vegetables (storytelling). The parent explains how eating vegetables will give the child more energy for playing (presenting benefits). The child, inspired by the athletes and the superhero story, becomes more open to eating vegetables.

Examples from Renowned Companies

Apple Inc. - Creating Scarcity
Apple often uses scarcity to drive demand for their products. During product launches, Apple limits the availability of their new products, creating long lines and high demand (scarcity). Showcasing customers who camp out overnight to buy the latest iPhone influences others to do the same (social proof). Apple's reputation as a leader in technology drives people to trust their product recommendations (authority). This strategy creates a buzz and urgency, resulting in high sales and media coverage.

Amazon - Social Proof and Reciprocity
Amazon uses customer reviews and personalized recommendations to persuade purchases. Displaying customer reviews and ratings helps new customers feel confident about their purchase decisions (social proof). Offering personalized recommendations based on previous purchases makes customers feel valued and understood (reciprocity). Highlighting limited-time deals and stock availability encourages quicker purchasing decisions (scarcity). These tactics enhance customer trust and drive more sales.

Nike - Building Rapport and Authority
Nike uses athletes and influencers to endorse their products. The use of famous athletes in advertisements ensures that Nike is associated with excellent high-performance sportswear (authority). By

exposing the public to athletes' interesting personal stories, failures, and challenges, Nike establishes a strong emotional relationship with its audience (liking). Emphasizing the fact that superstars wear Nike products encourages fans and future athletes to do the same (social proof). The influence of Nike's awesome persuasion on consumer branding loyalty assures considerable sales.

Chapter 7
Creating Lasting Positive Impact

Real-world companies have strategies that help them positively influence customers. They are focused on great value through the delivery of high-quality products and services, going beyond what customers expect from them. They also care about important issues like being kind to the environment and treating workers fairly, which may make customers feel good about supporting them. For instance, companies use sustainable materials, give back to the community, and reduce waste in their operations to indicate that they are in tandem with socially conscious customers.

Companies may rely on big ideas, but even cleverer tricks make them attention-grabbing and sustain viewers' interests. For example, their ads and websites appear more vividly colored with eye-candy pictures. They have some stories that help people reminisce or bring about an exciting feeling of happiness while developing attachment to the brand name. They even use data to tailor their messages to make you feel that they really know you. And have you ever seen those little badges or stickers that say things like "bestseller" or "top-rated"? Those are there to tell you that other people love their stuff, too.

Sometimes, they'll even try to make you feel that you have to act really fast, with limited offers or exclusive deals. Not to forget the fun stuff- companies love to create experiences that make you feel like you are part of something special, like playing a game online or trying virtual reality. Using these strategies companies can grab your attention, make you feel good about supporting them, and keep coming back for more. Cool, right?

Real-life examples of influential persuasion

Let us consider how businesses implement various techniques of persuasion in their operations.

The Case of Amazon's One-Click Purchase

Amazon's One-Click Purchase is a perfect example of utilizing persuasion techniques and the thrust towards convenience on the side of the consumer. This concept first came into view in 1997, when Amazon tried to make it easy to sell its products. One-Click Purchase was the brainchild of Jeff Bezos, Amazon's CEO, which would make the checkout process smoother for users and provide a better buying experience. By finishing transactions with a click, One-Click Purchase changed the face of online retailing, raising the benchmark in efficiency and user experience. The arrival of One-Click Purchase was one of the significant milestones that the company had to achieve; it showed that Amazon would go to any extent for innovation and customer satisfaction. Since it securely stored payment and shipping information, One-Click Purchase removed the need for redundant data entry, making it more convenient for the user. Amazon has continued to improve and optimize the feature by leveraging technology and consumer insights for impulse buying and fostering brand loyalty.

One-click purchase is an essential part of the setup for Amazon's effectiveness, showing that the company is committed to excellence in digital retail. As consumers increasingly want things easy and frictionless, Amazon's innovation creates a future for online shopping that will be seriously high for competition in the e-commerce space.

Nike's Emotional Branding

Nike's emotional branding strategy, deeply ingrained in its historical narrative, aligns very neatly with the tenets of persuasion through human emotions to create lasting relationships with customers and influence their purchase decisions. The late 1980s witnessed Nike's memorable "Just Do It" campaign, marking a significant milestone in the branding journey of the company. Born out of collaborative brainstorming sessions with Nike's advertising partner, Wieden+Kennedy, the slogan embodied Nike's very essence of empowerment, perseverance, and determination like those of athletes and people who need to overcome challenges. Thus, this emotionally charged message reached the masses' hearts, pushing them into the Nike brand as a source of inspiration and achievement.

Michael Jordan, basketball icon

Through the partnership with this basketball icon, Nike's powerful persuasive impact was further amplified. Initiated in 1984 with the introduction of the "Air Jordan" basketball shoes, this collaboration revolutionized sports marketing and celebrity endorsements. By associating the brand with Jordan's unmatched talent and charisma, Nike capitalized on principles of authority and social proof, convincing consumers of the brand's excellence in athletic performance and style. Over time, Nike has added quite a number of influential athletes and celebrities to its list; each has strategically been drawn into the company's books to influence its persuasive rhetoric.

Furthermore, Nike's commitment to social responsibility and purpose-driven initiatives has increased its persuasive power. Whether it is environmental sustainability or social justice and equality, Nike always aligns its brand with issues that resonate with consumers' values and convictions. Through authentic engagement in these dialogues and principled stands on significant matters, Nike strengthens its emotional bond with consumers, amplifying its persuasive allure and fostering brand allegiance.

Conclusion Nike's emotional branding agenda, woven into its history of effective campaigns, celebrity endorsements, and socially responsible efforts, integrates with persuasion principles to influence the consumer's behavior. Through compelling narratives, authentic experiences through the brand, and meaningful messaging, Nike inspires and equips the lives of millions worldwide and asserts itself as a leading provider in the industry of athletic apparel.

Starbuck's Loyalty Program

Starbucks' loyalty program is a prime example of how to use persuasion techniques to boost customer engagement and encourage repeat business. Rolled out in 2009, Starbucks Rewards has become vital to the company's success, keeping customers loyal through rewards, incentives, and personalized experiences.

In a nutshell, Starbucks' loyalty program depends on reciprocity, which is the 'key to persuasion.' The company provides rewards and perks for continuous support, so customers feel valued and are going to come again for more. This attracts the natural tendency to return kindness from customers, hence strengthening the relationship between Starbucks and its patrons.

Further, the Starbucks Rewards program relies on social proof to influence consumer behavior. By its tiered membership and special offers, the program makes membership a desirable and socially approved phenomenon. Members then experience a belonging and prestige that make them wish to join in and avail the benefits. Starbucks also lists the number of stars accumulated by each member, thereby starting a competition and challenging its customers to earn more stars.

Moreover, Starbucks Rewards makes participation more entertaining through gamification. It does this by giving stars for specific actions such as purchases or promotions. Starbucks converts the loyalty program into a fun, engaging experience by doing this. This encourages desired behavior while also building excitement through rewards.

In addition, Starbucks uses offer personalization and recommendation based on individual preferences and buying habits. Analysis of customer data enables Starbucks to send promotions or rewards that each member will find attractive, thereby enhancing the chances of repeat visits and high spending.

In the summary, Starbucks' loyalty program represents the proper application of persuasion techniques such as reciprocity, social proof, gamification, and personalization to promote customer loyalty and increases business growth. With these strategies, Apple has well connected itself to its customers and, thus, achieved long-term loyalty and success in a competitive market.

Apple's Product Design and Packaging

The perfect case study of using persuasion techniques in making the brand more attractive and driving consumer purchasing decisions would be Apple's product design and packaging. Since its inception in 1976, Apple has focused on design excellence, integrating persuasive elements into its products and packaging to capture consumers' imagination and differentiate itself in the market.

One of the persuasion techniques applied by Apple is the principle of aesthetics and simplicity. Starting with the Apple I computer, every product design had somehow managed to communicate with the market through clean lines, minimalism, and intuitive interfaces, thus embodying elegance and sophistication. This aesthetic emphasis directly appeals to consumer demand for sleek and stylish products and will influence their perceptions about quality and desirability. Moreover, the emphasis on simplicity in product design and packaging is enhanced with usability and a sense of ease and accessibility, further strengthening the persuasive appeal of Apple's products.

Social proof is another way in which Apple influences consumer behavior. The strategic marketing and product placement by Apple create a sense of exclusivity and desirability around its products, thus making them must-haves for tech-savvy consumers. The status symbols give off a sense of belonging to the Apple ecosystem and identifying with the brand. Such social proof creates a feeling among its users, which can lead to loyalty and even advocacy for the brand.

Moreover, the product packaging of Apple products goes into much detail to evoke positive emotional responses and an unforgettable unboxing. High-quality material and innovative structural design with minute attention to detail increases the perceived value of the product or, for that matter, the whole brand experience. The anticipation and emotions triggered through the unboxing process tap into the consumers' emotions for a delightful or satisfaction feeling which is an enhancement to the relationship between the consumer and the brand.

The product design and packing of Apple itself emphasize the storytelling and branding for a comprehensive brand narrative.

This isn't limited only to the packaging, where every little detail is counted to reinforce the identity and values of the brand. By integrating its products and packaging with a compelling brand story, Apple communicates with consumers on an emotional level, binding them even more closely to the brand.

In brief, the designing of the product and its packaging by Apple proved itself to be an excellent application of persuasion techniques in brand appeal and consumer-purchasing decisions. Apple makes aesthetics for social proof and emotional engagement such that it tells a story with the various products and packaging it designs, promoting loyalty and advocacy in this competitive world.

Uber's Surge Pricing

Uber's surge pricing strategy epitomizes the use of persuasion tactics for efficient supply and demand control. Since 2012, surge pricing, or dynamic pricing, has been adopted by Uber to change the rate at which it offers rides on a real-time basis through changes in demand and supply in a particular place.

Surge pricing, basically, is founded on the principle of scarcity-the very fundamental principle used in persuasion. It increases its prices at peak hours, including rush hours or inclement weather, when there are not enough drivers during such instances. In effect, Uber informs riders of lack by charging higher fares, creating a sensation that things are in short supply. The urgency elicited prompts the rider to book before prices rise further and things go out of stock. Such will have raised ride bookings, hence supply and demand will be balanced much better.

Furthermore, surge pricing includes a piece of social proof to drive passenger decisions. The transparent and effective presentation of surge multipliers in the Uber app during peak demand conditions provides riders with the impression that other passengers are willing to pay a higher price for their ride. This social proof influences passenger behavior by creating value in perceptions and desirability and encouraging passengers to pay willingness-to-pay prices by demonstrating that others are too willing to pay. Further, surge price on the application reinforces that Uber is the service most in demand and more desirable to customers.

Secondly, the loss aversion principle drives consumer's decision when Uber is adopting a strategy on its surge pricing. By framing surge pricing as a temporary increase in fares due to high demand, Uber creates a fear of missing out (FOMO) among passengers who may hesitate to book rides at regular prices. The prospect of missing out on a ride or higher prices in the future keeps passengers on board and accepting surge pricing by securing transportation immediately to avoid a complete loss on missing a ride.

In a nutshell, Uber's surge pricing strategy implements effective persuasion techniques such as scarcity, social proof, and loss aversion in managing supply and demand dynamics. Through these principles, Uber is able to push passengers to book rides at peak demand periods, thus striking a balance between supply and demand and creating more revenue-generating opportunities for drivers. In the final analysis, surge pricing will allow Uber to offer its customers transportation at the exact time they require it, thus improving satisfaction and loyalty toward the brand.

These case studies demonstrate how companies use clever tricks such as making it easier to buy, playing on emotions, focusing on looks, rewarding loyalty, and dynamic pricing to achieve their goals and succeed. So, the next time you go shopping or use a service, watch out for these techniques in action-they might just persuade you to make that purchase or stick with a brand!

Strategies for leaving a lasting positive impression on others

Following are the keys to persuading others to leave a lasting positive impression on others:

Active Listening and Empathy: Active listening and empathy form the foundation blocks of great communication, laying the very bedrock strong relationships are built on. At their core, they necessitate more than just hearing the words-they demand an authentic understanding of the emotions, perspectives, and experiences that people carry into a conversation.

Active listening is not just nodding along and waiting to get your say in. It is all attention, both verbal and nonverbal, on the speaker. Eye contact, nodding, or another affirmation gesture should be communicated through verbal cues, such as when you paraphrase or summarize what has been said. Such participation in a conversation shows respect for a speaker and their opinion.

Empathic listening goes beyond the above act of active listening and will delve to a stage of understanding not only what the speaker is saying but how they feel about it. The need to tune into both their words and body language, putting yourself in the speaker's shoes, to be able to imagine how you might feel in their position. By empathizing with this speaker, you build a safe space where they are heard, understood, and validated.

This develops trust and a connection because empathetic listening tells the speaker that their feelings are important to you. If a person is really listened to and understood, they are more likely to open up and share their thoughts and feelings honestly. This can lead to more meaningful interactions and stronger bonds, as it allows for deeper levels of communication and connection to occur.

What such empathetic listening looks like in practical terms could be to reflect back the speaker's emotions; ask open-ended questions to push them further about these feelings; validate their experiences without judgment but allow it to play out and set aside your agenda for the conversation.

Example: The customer service representative at Zappos listens to what a customer has to say concerning a late delivery, empathizes with the frustration, offers a sincere apology along with a resolution, and shows the customer that they matter.

Confidence and Authenticity: Assurance in interactions serves as a cornerstone for establishing confidence and credibility in both personal and professional relationships. It's not just about projecting confidence for the sake of appearances but about embodying real authenticity and sincerity in every interaction.

When you approach interactions with assurance, you convey a sense of self-assurance that is palpable to those around you. This assurance stems from a deep understanding and acceptance of yourself, your values, and your abilities. It's about being comfortable in your own skin and having confidence in your thoughts, actions, and decisions.

Authenticity is the key to developing closer relationships. When you are authentic and honest in your communication with others, they will easily trust and believe you and connect meaningfully with you. It is about being true and genuine to yourself, expressing openly your thoughts, feelings, or beliefs. Authenticity should not pretend to be what you do not really feel or hide behind a mask to appease others.

Being authentic creates an environment of trust and openness wherein others feel comfortable being themselves. Authenticity in relationships creates strong bonds by fostering mutual respect, understanding, and acceptance. When people get a feeling that you are genuine and sincere, they are more open to opening up to you and sharing their thoughts, feelings, and concerns.

In addition, authenticity enhances your power because honesty and sincerity in your words and deeds will always shine through. The moment you speak and act with authenticity, people are bound to listen to what you have to say and do as you instruct them. This is because authenticity breeds credibility, meaning that the moment others believe that you are genuine and honest, they will easily place their trust in your judgment and respect your opinion.

The key to inspiring trust in other people is staying true to oneself and speaking your thoughts and beliefs with confidence. Confidence in yourself stems from knowing who you are, what you stand for, and what you are capable of achieving. You will inspire confidence in other people, and you will present yourself as a reliable and trustworthy person, by speaking confidently about who you are.

Example: Steve Jobs' confident and authentic style of presentation at Apple product launch events where he passionately elaborates on innovations while acknowledging previous mistakes resonates with audiences and enhances the reputation of Apple as an innovator and transparent brand.

Persuasive Language: The use of clear, concise, and respectful language is the basis of effective communication. The more you explain your thoughts in simple terms, the more likely others are to fully understand and engage with your thoughts. Clarity ensures that your message is easily understood, leaving little room for misinterpretation or confusion.

This also helps with conciseness, wherein you are able to say your message in a short yet effective way without loading the audience with too much information or verbosity. You condense the essence of your message to its most potent form and capture your audience's attention while keeping it on the right track concerning what you want to communicate to them.

Respectful language is the backbone of good communication. It sets the atmosphere of mutual understanding and consideration. When you use words that are inclusive and respectful of other people's opinion, you are showing respect to their points of view and opinions. Respectful communication opens up a two-way dialogue and cooperation and leads to effective interaction and true relationships.

Besides clarity, conciseness, and respectfulness, deploying persuasive language techniques can be an added advantage to communicate well. The use of storytelling helps illustrate vivid points and be able to talk on emotional levels with people. Whenever you use stories to communicate, you are giving your audience experiences to remember, which in turn touches their sensibilities and inspires them to action.

Appealing to emotions is the most powerful persuasive technique in changing attitudes and behavior. You can evoke a sense of empathy, compassion, or excitement in your audience by tapping into their emotions, making them connect to your message on a deeper level. Emotionally resonant communication not only captures attention but also fosters lasting engagement and commitment.

Mastering persuasive language gives you the power to express thoughts persuasively and to motivate action in others. Whether you are presenting, leading a team, or just one-on-one, you can persuade other people toward a certain outcome and create some meaningful change. With impressive communication skills and persuasive techniques, you can make others consider your ideas, support your initiatives, and work with you toward common goals.

Example: Nike's "Just Do It" slogan effectively communicates a message of empowerment and determination, inspiring athletes and consumers worldwide to overcome challenges and pursue their goals with confidence and determination.

Highlight Shared Values and Common Goals: The ability to understand common values with others is required in establishing solid connections as well as in nurturing mutual understanding for building good relationships. This leads to meaning relationships, thereby generating the feeling of unity and collaboration on the basis of mutual trust.

Shared values are that common ground on which people can meet and relate to one another. When you identify similar goals and aspirations, then you have a sense of belonging and camaraderie. By acknowledging shared values, you validate the beliefs and principles that are important to both parties, establishing a strong sense of mutual respect and understanding.

Emphasizing shared values cultivates a supportive environment where individuals feel valued and appreciated for who they are. When people feel that their values align with those of their peers, it fosters a sense of belonging and inclusivity. This sense of unity creates a supportive ecosystem where everyone feels empowered to contribute their unique perspectives and talents towards a common goal.

Moreover, shared goals and aspirations are a good reason for cooperation and synergy. When people are united by a common goal, they are more inspired to collaborate and work towards common goals. By emphasizing common objectives, you inspire a collective sense of purpose and direction, driving individuals to work together towards achieving meaningful outcomes.

In practical terms, it would be recognizing shared values as active listening and seeking to understand others' perspectives and beliefs. This requires empathy and an openness to other viewpoints so that you can engage in meaningful dialogue and collaborate. It demonstrates a willingness to connect at a deeper level and build trust-based relationships by acknowledging and respecting others' values.

Additionally, shared values and objectives tend to enhance a sense of responsibility and commitment within the group. When everyone is working together toward a common vision, accountability is fostered. Everyone holds themselves and each other accountable for the accomplishment of shared goals. This sense of responsibility enhances the bonding among members of the team and promotes an excellent culture and constant improvement.

Example: Patagonia is aligned with the interests of the target audience to ensure that the values created are the same. Among various initiatives such as "1% for the Planet", the brand also advocates to keep the environment intact. End.

Appreciation and Thankfulness: Showing gratitude to others' contribution is not only courtesy but it is an element of nurturing positive and harmonious relations. It transcends from politeness, it becomes recognition and acknowledgment of people's efforts and input that helps build a respect-filled, acknowledgement, and appreciative culture.

When you say you are grateful, you communicate that they have spent time, effort, and energy on doing their job or in connecting with you. It validates their efforts so that they feel important or valued within the context of being part of the team or the relationship. It communicates your appreciation to them for the efforts they put in not only to be noticed but appreciated and respected.

In addition, true gratitude reinforces interpersonal relationships. Whenever people are appreciated and recognized, there is a sense of goodwill and reciprocity. They will be much more likely to be positive toward you and will want to continue making meaningful contributions. Reinforcing positive behavior contributes to building trust and rapport and lays the groundwork for deeper and more fulfilling relationships.

Apart from bonding, gratitude creates a positive environment where individuals feel appreciated and motivated to excel. When people know that their efforts are appreciated, they boost their morale and feel a sense of belonging. They feel valued for their unique talents and contributions, which in turn encourages them to continue striving for excellence.

In addition, appreciation and gratitude work as building blocks of a collaborative culture and teamwork. Appreciation by the team members inspires individuals toward a cooperation-based spirit. They are more likely to collaborate with their peers to share knowledge and skills and to work toward common goals. This collaborative environment fuels innovation and productivity within any team or organization.

Example: Starbucks' "Pay It Forward" campaign encourages customers to buy coffee for the person in line behind them, creating a chain of kindness and fostering a sense of community and gratitude among customers, ultimately leaving a positive impression of the Starbucks brand.

These examples from real life show how persuasion strategies can really make a difference in leaving a lasting positive impression on others in different situations.

Chapter Eight
Persuasion Alchemy in the Digital Age

If we start from the very basic, Persuasion in the digital age relies on a blend of traditional techniques and modern digital strategies. Here's a closer look:

1. Knowledge of Your Audience: Digital persuasion doesn't depend on the gut feeling. Instead, you use data to make sense of it so that you understand who your target audience is in terms of demographics, preferences, and behavior, which helps you in building an appeal according to their concern and interest.

2. Personalization: Digital platforms can enable content and experiences to become more personalized according to a person's preferences and his behavior. From personalized emails to customized product recommendations or targeted ads, it allows the audience to experience something in relevance and engagement that is likely to persuade them in turn.

3. Engagement Strategies: Digital channels are very open for engagement opportunities such as interactive content, social media, etc. Involving the audience by quiz, polls, contests or live streams is not only attracting but creating a two-way dialogue that creates trust and relationship, making persuasion so effective.

4. Visual Content: In the virtual world, visuals are key attention-grabbers and great ways to convey messages rapidly and effectively. Compelling images, videos, and infographics in your digital content boost its persuasive power, making it more memorable and engaging to your audience.

5. Storytelling: This is a means of persuasion that is even with the advancement of the digital age. You can reach into a deeper connection and even create empathy by weaving some narratives that resonate with the experiences and emotions of the audience and thus your message becomes persuasive and memorable.

6. Social proof: Social proof, reviews, testimonials, and social media endorsements are huge influential factors of digital persuasion. Through social proof, credibility and trust are created in the minds of the audience of the message and it creates an acceptance and take action toward the claim.

7. Conversational Marketing: With the arrival of chatbots and messaging apps, conversational marketing has become increasingly significant in digital persuasion. It allows for real-time conversations with your audience, meaning you can answer questions or concerns they may have directly and create understanding and guide them toward conversion.

8. Continuous Optimization: Digital persuasion is an iterative process. You have to keep optimizing and refining it by testing various strategies, analyzing data, and adjusting according to performance for it to become effective with the passage of time.

Adapting Ancient Wisdom to Modern Communication Trends

Adapting ancient wisdom to modern communication in real life deals with applying timeless principles and insights gained in the past towards navigating the problems and interactions of the contemporary. Here's how:

1. Mindfulness and Presence: Traditional wisdom has a lot to do with mindfulness and presence in communication. Fully being present in a conversation-whether it's face-to-face or online-can really add so much to understanding and connection. Such practices as active listening, non-verbal cues, and focused attention help to achieve real engagement and empathy.

For example, when designing its products and doing its marketing, Apple infuses mindfulness in it. Apple's intuitive products encourage the user to remain focused on what they are trying to do without distraction; for example, Apple's device "Do Not Disturb" feature lets a user set notifications to be silent during specific times or periods thus ensuring minimal disturbance and providing more mindful usage with increased productivity.

2. Emotional Intelligence: The ancient philosophies often stress emotional intelligence where it is understood that how emotions must be understood and handled for interpersonal communication. This gives way to empathetic listening wherein one acknowledges the emotions and validates them. Expressive skills are also effective, yet constructive in conveying the same feeling. Emotional intelligence helps in establishing sound relationships and facilitates resolution in conflicts.

For example, in Airbnb's "We Accept" campaign, it clearly exhibited emotional intelligence through the conversation about the sensitive issue of the 2017 travel ban in a compassionate and empathetic manner. In doing so, the campaign talked about values such as inclusiveness and acceptance, and those values really resonated with the audience and cemented Airbnb's reputation as championing social justice and human rights. Through this form of communication, Airbnb succeeded to connect emotionally with the customers, building understanding, empathy, and solidarity.

3. Storytelling Power: Storytelling has always been an essential part of human communication. Ancient myths, fables, and parables have entertained as well as communicated serious truths and moral lessons. Even in modern times, storytelling continues to be a powerful method for building relationships, for explaining complicated ideas, and for moving people to action. When they are able to develop compelling stories that stir the audience, communicators are likely to capture attention, to evoke emotions, and also move beliefs and behaviors.

For example, Nike has grasped the art of storytelling to connect emotionally with its audience. For example, "Just Do It" is one of the most powerful advertisements that inspires individuals to push their limits and get over their problems. For example, Nike collaborated with athlete Colin Kaepernick. In this case, the convincing narrative revolved around Kaepernick's resilience and determination in overcoming adversity, which sparked conversations and reached viewers all over the world.

4. Authenticity and Integrity: The authenticity and integrity of message is very important according to ancient thought. When trust is above everything in the world, genuineness and honesty toward each other create credibility in communications. Authentic communication lies in sticking to one's belief system, telling the truth with no malice, and keeping the word. Authenticity empowers people to have deeper connections and evoke confidence in each other.

Patagonia, being honest and truthful about commitment to environmental sustainability, exemplifies an ideal example of authentic communication with integrity. Patagonia is transparent about communicating its environmental and social responsibility initiatives, its promise toward fair labor practice and ethical sourcing. For example, in the recent advertising campaign by Patagonia under "Worn Wear", the brand encouraged repairing the customers' garment with repair kits, which reflected a brand that does not care to "consume and waste".

5. Practicing Empathy and Compassion: Many ancient viewpoints advocate for the practice of empathy and compassion towards others. In today's diverse and unified world, understanding and appreciating different perspectives is essential for effective communication. By cultivating understanding, individuals can bridge cultural and ideological divides, promote inclusivity, and foster mutual understanding and respect.

For instance, Google's communication reflects clearly the empathy and compassion by emphasizing the user experience and accessibility. Google is always seeking feedback from its users and integrates them with different features that meet diversified needs. For example, the "Accessibility" project at Google is centered on building inclusive and accessible products and services to reach all people regardless of the presence of disability.

6. Seeking the Wisdom of Elders and Mentors: An old-age culture often revered elders and the seeking of wisdom from seniors in one's community. Currently, obtaining guidance and mentorship from established professionals can come in the form of valuable ideas and visions. Mentors can also give advice, narrate experience, and guide individuals so that they better handle all complex communication requirements and undergo personal and professional change.

For instance: Starbucks fosters a sense of community and mentorship in its corporate culture as well as the customer experience. Starbucks empowers the baristas to befriend customers and colleagues; that brings about a sense of belongingness and supportiveness. For instance, the "Partner Open Forum" allows employees to present ideas, ask questions, and get insights from veteran colleagues, which is some form of seeking wisdom from elders and other mentors within the organization.

Leveraging Digital Platforms for Ethical Persuasion

Taking advantage of digital platforms for ethical persuasion means that one uses all the online channels and tools at his or her disposal in order to influence others responsibly, clearly, and within the realm of ethical value. Here's how you can do it:

1. Transparency and Honesty: Be open with your intentions and affiliations. If you are trying to sell a product, indicate any partnership or sponsorship deals. This helps your audience trust you and makes them knowledgeable about what they are buying.

Example: During its acquisition by The Coca-Cola Company, Honest Tea has shown a commitment to open and honest communication in that the company has really made a concerted effort to address complaints from customers. Honest Tea's co-founder Seth Goldman did not shy away from discussing the issue nor downplaying the significance of the acquisition; he interacted with customers.

The rationale and any ramification for the brand on the transaction were explained by Goldman in a letter posted on the business website and further spread through social media. He assured customers that Honest Tea would never compromise from its core values of fair trade sourcing, organic ingredient usage, and environmental sustainability.

In addition, Honest Tea continued to ensure transparency in labeling and packaging of its products to ensure that the consumer could obtain insightful information regarding the components of its products as well as the efforts the company makes toward environmental protection. Honest Tea was seeking credibility from its audience and letting the world know that it stood for truthfulness and honesty despite making drastic changes by retaining such transparency.

2. Respect for Privacy: Always respect people's privacy rights. Obtain consent before collecting personal data and give them control over how it's used. This fosters trust and maintains the integrity of your persuasion efforts.

For instance, Spotify is a global music streaming business that placed emphasis on transparency and user control over personal data. The company took extensive measures to comply with the new requirements after the GDPR was implemented in 2018. These measures included establishing explicit consent procedures for data collection, updating privacy rules to improve clarity and accessibility, and introducing features that would give users control over their privacy settings and usage of their data. The efforts demonstrate how the company upholds rights on privacy, guarantees its adherence to the GDPR, and also helps enhance its standing as a responsible user data custodian.

3. Informed Consent: Let people understand the consequences of what they do. Make them receive factual information rather than leading them into decisions under force or pressure. Then there would be consent in itself.

Example: Google is a global technology company that has high regard for allowing people to give their consent freely and be aware of the implications of their actions, especially with regard to privacy and data collection. Google gives its customers information about the types of data it collects, why it collects them, and privacy protections through transparent terms of service and privacy policies. With granular controls over privacy settings, Google provides the users with control to change their preferences for data across all of its services. There is transparent communication in ensuring that users are informed of policy changes. Openness and informed consent that Google uses build relationships with people and improve trust.

4. Empowerment and Autonomy: Assist the individual in making choices based on accurate information and their values. Educate them through digital platforms so they can make decisions that are aligned with their best interests.

Example: The non-profit educational organization Khan Academy provides free online tutorials and information on a variety of subjects. Khan Academy offers individualized learning experiences through its digital platform based on the objectives and skill levels of its students. For students, there will be access to practice questions, instructional videos, and ways to track progress. Because of this freedom, by being allowed to make choices that suit their interests, students will learn at their own pace. This is especially so in cases where using Khan Academy helps students arrive at the correct information by developing critical thinking skills.

5. Avoid Manipulation and Coercion: Never employ fraudulent tactics. Use truth, sincerity, and a consideration of a person's rights as an alternative basis for influence tactics.

Example: Because Ben & Jerry's commits to using only Fairtrade-certified ingredients, farmers and laborers will get fair compensation, secure working conditions, and environmentally sustainable products. The company supports communities in developing nations and promotes fair labor practices through giving priority to Fairtrade coffee, vanilla, and cocoa. This commitment further represents Ben & Jerry's leadership in the food industry on the use of ethical sourcing and is in line with the company's ideals of social justice and sustainability.

6. Promoting Well-being and Social Good: Focus on promoting well-being and social good rather than exploiting vulnerabilities. Align your persuasive efforts with ethical values and principles.

Example: Sustainability and environmental responsibility are top priorities for Seventh Generation, a business that specializes in personal care and household products.

The company prioritizes cutting waste, lowering its carbon footprint, and employing plant-based materials. Seventh Generation has come up with products, eco-friendly in nature, with regard to consumers and encourages environment stewardship through conducting a morally based business. This approach by the enterprise allows making other companies more mindful regarding their ecologically friendlier methodologies and makes for good constructive contributions toward favoring environmental consequences for generations coming after.

7. Accountability and Responsibility: Be accountable and responsive to your actions and its consequences. Monitor the outcomes of your persuasion and respond accordingly to ensure that they are ethical. For example, through a variety of initiatives, the global beverage company Coca-Cola demonstrates an accountability for its water use and how it impacts nearby communities and ecosystems.

Through efforts such as reforestation and wetland restoration, the company engages local communities and conservation organizations to rejuvenate the water supplies.

Coca-Cola conducts assessments of the risks posed by water to identify areas of development and minimize its impact on the environment. By monitoring its use of water and assuming responsibility for it, Coca-Cola shows its commitment to environmental sustainability and responsible water stewardship.

Chapter Nine
Emerging Trends and Persuasion

Advances in technology and changing social standards are driving constant change in the field of persuasion. In this chapter, we will observe the new developments and trends influencing persuasion. We will explore the novel ways in which artificial intelligence, data analytics, social media, and behavioral science are being used to impact choices and actions. Through real-world examples, we will demonstrate the useful uses and ramifications of these trends using actual cases.

1. The role of artificial intelligence in persuasion.

The field of AI is transforming our ability to understand and influence human behavior, which has the potential of processing huge data sets using algorithms that can find patterns and predict outcomes, offering the opportunity for highly targeted and potent persuasion strategies.

Example: virtual assistants and chatbots

With the artificial intelligence, companies such as Google and Amazon can have virtual assistants like Alexa or Google Assistant that can talk with clients in natural language. Depending on user information and interests, these assistants will offer customized suggestions, indicate items, and influence a purchasing decision. For instance, if the user requests a recipe through Alexa, it might suggest some ingredients with particular brands and subtly encourage the user to make purchases. Such interaction brings more possibilities of engaging a user in making purchases while offering timely, relevant, and convenient recommendations.

2. Data-Driven Personalization

Thanks to Data Analytics that Influencers and marketers can create customized messages based on the tastes, wants, and habits of specific consumers. Persuasive messages are more relevant and successful when they are personalized.

Example: The Netflix's recommendation system

Netflix analyzes user preferences and watching history using complex algorithms to suggest TV series and films. Customers are more satisfied and devoted when they receive a tailored approach that keeps them interested and impacts their watching decisions. Netflix keeps viewers engaged and promotes binge-watching by spotting what they would want to watch next. This has a direct effect on viewer retention rates and membership renewals. For example, when a user watches crime dramas on Netflix, the algorithm favors similar genres in its suggestions, which improves the user's experience and caters to their preferences.

3. Behavioural economics and nudge theory

Main objectives of Behavioral Economics and Nudge theory are to comprehend and generate revenue from the cognitive biases as well as heuristics used in human decision-making. People can be nudged toward desirable actions by creating settings and options that support certain biases.

Example: Policies for Organ Donation

Opt-out organ donation laws have been enacted in nations like the UK and Spain, where people are automatically regarded as donors unless they indicate a different preference. By utilizing the default effect bias, this policy design—which is based on the nudge theory—has dramatically raised the rates of organ donation. The opt-out model's simplicity increases the likelihood that people will continue to donate, expanding the pool of organs available for transplantation. This strategy differs from opt-in systems, which require contributors to voluntarily register, frequently leading to less participation rates due to inertia and procrastination.

4. The Power of Social Media Influencers

A new generation of influencers has developed – thanks to social media platforms, and they have incredible persuasive control over their following. By sharing relatable and real material, these influencers have the power to affect attitudes, actions, and trends.

Example: Kylie Jenner and Cosmetic Sales

Using her enormous online following, social media influencer Kylie Jenner has effectively developed a billion-dollar cosmetics industry. Her product endorsements and marketing have a significant and direct influence on what customers decide to buy. She establishes a sense of authenticity and trust that traditional advertising frequently lacks by demonstrating her own use of the items. Sales and brand loyalty soar when Kylie uses her own lip kits to create a lesson, which her fans interpret as a sincere recommendation.

5. Immersive Technologies: VR and AR

Immersion and interactive persuasive experiences are being made possible by advances in virtual reality (VR) and augmented reality (AR) technologies. These technologies have the power to arouse intense emotions and leave a lasting impact.

Example: IKEA Place App

With the use of their smartphone and the IKEA Place augmented reality software, individuals can see furniture in their home. This immersive experience affects customer's purchase decisions because it helps customers see how things fit and appear in their area. The ability to digitally arrange furniture in a home reduces uncertainty and increases the likelihood that a sale will be made. For example, if a consumer is not sure of the size and color of the couch that would fit in his living room, he can use an app to see it and boost his confidence in making the right choice.

6. The Rise of Micro-Influencers

In the persuasion world, a micro-influencer, someone with a small yet very engaged following, has been popularized. They are quite successful in influencing niche markets because of their perceived genuineness and stronger relationship with their audience.

Example: Niche Fitness Influencers

Influencers in the fitness industry who possess particular knowledge in fields like CrossFit, yoga, or vegan diet may greatly influence the buying decisions of their followers. Within their narrow groups, they may influence customer preferences and increase sales by recommending particular brands or items. An influencer in the vegan fitness space, for example, may advocate for plant-based protein powders and persuade their followers to select them over alternatives made of animal products. Their audience develops a sense of trust and dependability thanks to their in-depth assessments and first-hand testimonies.

7. Ethical Considerations and Transparency

Transparency and ethical issues become increasingly crucial as persuasion strategies get more complex. To keep integrity and trust, persuasive techniques must respect people's right to privacy and autonomy.

Example: GDPR and Data Privacy

The General Data Protection Regulation of the European Union necessitates strict conditions on data privacy and consent. Companies should be transparent with customers on how they gather and use their personal information, and the customers should be in charge of it. The rule has to do with prioritizing the rights of users and privacy, thus promoting ethical persuasion. Any company that does not follow the rules is likely to face severe penalties, emphasizing the importance of moral principles to persuasive strategies.

For example, a company gathering the data of users with its intention of using it in order to influence targeted ads need to attain explicit approval and allow their consumers to 'opt out'.

Technological breakthrough, data-related insights, as well as gaining a better understanding about humans' behaviour are giving ways to form the future of persuasion. As these tendencies continue to grow, it will become crucial to balance effectiveness with morals in building credibility and support for favorable outcomes. Through the use of AI, personalization, social media, immersion technology, and behavioral research, we can create compelling approaches that are both powerful and respectful of people's privacy and autonomy. In the future, moral conducts should be monitored so as to ensure that the persuasive means will benefit society.

Chapter Ten
Mastering Persuasion: A Lifelong Journey

This complex world of human connections places persuasion as one of the most powerful and transformative skills we can acquire. Starting from the early childhood days when we first learn to articulate our needs and negotiate with those around us, it is the power of persuasion that continues determining our experiences and consequences up through the difficult negotiations and debates of adulthood. This chapter represents a culmination of insights, strategies, and real-world applications explored in this book. It is also a reflective journey we all undertake to become the most effective communicators and influencers.

Persuasion is at its core not manipulation, nor deceit. It has to do with understanding perspectives and motivations of others to present our ideas in the light of their values and aspirations. It has to do with building trust, fostering empathy, and creating connections that reach beyond superficial differences. Through these stories, examples, and lessons in this book, we have seen how master persuaders operate-how they listen, adapt, and communicate with clarity and conviction.

Developing a Lifelong Commitment to Mastering Persuasion

Throughout life, we encounter innumerable situations where persuasion is applied. Whether persuading a friend to stand with a particular cause, a colleague at work to accept a different approach, or even to personally motivate ourselves towards reaching various goals, persuasion plays the ultimate role. However, only through dedication and the acceptance of continuous learning and changes can one cultivate lifelong development in mastering the art of persuasion. The journey is quite dynamic, showing our growing nature and the changing situations in which we communicate. This commitment involves constant hone-up of our skills; seeking feedback, and having opportunities to practice and get better at techniques.

Consider the story of Dr. Paul Farmer, a physician and renowned anthropologist. Dr. Farmer has worked throughout his career to push for greater access to health care by poor communities. His case-making was not just made in facts and figures, but also through personal tales of patients he had interacted with. By humanizing the issue and showing genuine compassion, he was able to gain support from diverse groups of people, from government officials to philanthropists. Dr. Farmer's work is a great example of the power of a lifetime commitment to persuasion. In his ability to adapt a message to different audiences, yet remain true to his cause, he has been making a difference in global health.

It means a mind-set of constant improvement: being open to learning the skills and perfecting them at every given moment in any conversation, because it's just one opportunity after another. That is where commitment in mastering persuasion shows, when taking on every persuasive opportunity, not as a win or conquer, but to connect, understand, and influence meaningfully.

For example, consider the case of Steve Jobs. Steve Jobs is one of the founders of Apple Inc. Steve was a visionary and a persuader extraordinaire. His presentations, especially when he was unveiling new products, were almost legendary in capturing the audience and creating great enthusiasm among consumers. Steve worked tirelessly to hone his presentations, showing just how committed he was to perfecting the art of persuasion. His simplicity to express how Apple's product would be very innovative and functional had helped bring the brand of Apple forward in the marketplace. And that is one of the points of Jobs' travel through the realms of persuasion.

Continual Growth in Influence and Positive Impact

It's a journey, really, about both personal growth and a positive impact we have on other people. In learning how to better influence, one is also capable of positively influencing the world around us-in our communities, our workplaces, our personal lives. Persuasion practiced ethically, with integrity, is not only useful in helping others understand an issue but in conflict resolution and even inspiration for change.

An excellent example is Malala Yousafzai, the young activist for girls' education. Surviving a brutal attack by the Taliban, Malala continued to advocate for education with even greater enthusiasm. Her speeches and writings are powerful because they combine logical arguments with personal narrative and emotional appeal. Malala's persuasive communication has mobilized the entire world to support her cause. This has led to increased funding for education initiatives and raised awareness of the issues that girls face worldwide. Her influence and positive impact are a testament to the power of continual growth in persuasion.

Continued influence building calls for awareness of the ethics behind our persuasive endeavors. This involves a responsibility, through the use of such skills, to ensure a basis of trust is constructed and authentic relationships built between parties. In so doing, we not only reap our rewards but help the other person achieve their's as well, spreading into a wave of influence to affect change.

We find leaders like Satya Nadella, the CEO of Microsoft, who transformed the company's culture by fostering a growth mind set and emphasizing empathy and collaboration. Nadella's approach to persuasion involves listening to employees, understanding their concerns, and aligning his vision with the values of his employees. His commitment to continuous learning and adaptation has not only revitalized Microsoft but also inspired a more inclusive and innovative work environment.

Through the entire book, we learned that persuasion is a very broad phenomenon. We saw it work in the context of interpersonal relations and in professional spheres. The use of public speaking as well as in private dialogue is demonstrated in every context. With each chapter comes tools and strategies to be used for more effective persuasion, effective communication, and respectful and empathetic influence on others.

And so, as we close in on the end of this trip, let's not forget that persuasion is more than a technique to be acquired; it's a means of interacting with the world. It is about paying attention to what others require and want, and working with your skills to do good. Irrespective of the group one aspires to influence or seek change across larger sections, these principles and practices by such will set a guide on the ropes to navigate through human communications.

Activity Session: Implementing Persuasion in Business Plans

Objective: To help new-business owners integrate persuasive techniques into their business strategies to attract investors, partners, and customers.

Step 1: Identifying Your Audience

- Identify the key stakeholders: investors, customers, partners.

- Research their values, needs, and concerns.

Step 2: Crafting Your Message

- Ethos: Establish credibility. Highlight your expertise, experience, and ethical commitment. For example, if you're starting a tech company, share your experience in technology and any prosperous projects you've operated.

- Pathos: Appeal to emotions. Share a persuasive story that exemplifies the problem your business resolves. For instance, if you're launching a healthcare product, tell a story about how it positively impacted a real person's life.

- Logos: Use reason and statistics. Provide clear, reasoned arguments with data to back your claims. Bring forward market research, potential ROI, and case studies that will make people believe you.

Step 3: Leverage Reciprocity

- Provide upfront value. This may come in the form of free service, valuable information, or even a discount. Use your new software launch as an example by giving early adopters free service for one month.

Step 4: Leverage Social Proof

- Collect testimonials and endorsements. Present beta tester or early customer feedback. Try to obtain endorsement from some popular figures in your business.

Step 5: Scarcity

- Limited-time offers and exclusive offers. Use an offer for the first 100 customers, for example, or an exclusive package for early investors.

Step 6: Authority

- Expert endorsements. If industry experts and credible organizations endorse your product, let everyone know by writing this on your presentations or marketing materials.

Step 7: Rehearsals of Delivery

- Practice scenarios. Role-playing pitches with potential investors and customers with peers or mentors yields great feedback on delivery and what should be improved.

Example Exercise: Pitch Practice

- Split into pairs. One person plays the role of the business owner, and the other plays the role of an investor or customer.

- The business owner delivers their pitch, incorporating ethos, pathos, logos, reciprocity, social proof, scarcity, and authority.

- The partner provides feedback on strengths and areas for improvement.

- Switch roles and repeat.

Reflection:

- After the exercise, gather in small groups to discuss what techniques were most effective and why.

- Share insights and strategies on how to refine pitches and presentations.

With these persuasion techniques now an integral part of their business plan, new-business owners will then be able to communicate better, build trust with the stakeholder, and drive their business into success. As we close this chapter and this book, remember that the art of mastering persuasion is a never-ending journey. Continue to learn, practice, and apply these principles, and your ability to influence and inspire will grow, and ultimately lead to greater personal and professional fulfillment.

Concluding thoughts by the Author

Thank you for joining us on this exploration of persuasion. May these lessons here make you an even more effective communicator, strengthen your relationships, and achieve your goals with a confident heart and compassion.

Let's just try to see it with an example of Martin Luther King Jr.'s power. The greatest example of persuasive communication is his "I Have a Dream" speech. The man, Martin Luther King Jr., so masterfully expressed his vision for racial equality and justice in his use of a blend of emotional appeal, ethical appeal, and logical argument, and this has inspired millions of people to move and sparked big social change. His commitment to nonviolent persuasion and continuous growth in his methods of influence created a lasting impact that continues to inspire and guide movements for justice and equality around the world.

Similarly, in the corporate world, think about Howard Schultz as the former CEO of Starbucks, who, through his forceful leadership, made Starbucks, once an insignificant coffee chain, transform into a global brand.

He emphasized the importance of creating a unique customer experience and building a community within the coffeehouse environment. Schultz is able to win both the hearts of his employees and his customers at Starbucks to appreciate the experience. His story epitomizes the importance of creating a bond and real connections toward achieving lasting influence.

By and large, you can represent all this in your personal and professional lives. Persuading the team of a new approach that you adopt, convincing your client why your services mean value for them, even negotiating what roles and responsibilities everybody should get in your family, master persuasion skills can truly play you well on all these accounts; always maintain integrity, compassion and a keen interest in and rapport with the other party to whom you are persuading.

As we close the last chapter, let us accept the journey of mastering persuasion as a lifelong pursuit. This is a journey that will require dedication, reflection, and a constant willingness to learn and grow. By so doing, we enhance not only our abilities but also contribute to a more connected and understanding world.